The
Woodcock

ARTISTS' IMPRESSIONS

The Woodcock

ARTISTS' IMPRESSIONS

SWAN·HILL
PRESS

Of all the wild game birds, the woodcock has a place of its own. Unpredictable, secretive, virtually invisible on the ground, wonderfully erratic in flight, and a serious challenge to any marksman. It is also a valued prize for bird-watchers. As a, largely, migratory species, its arrival and departure provides seasonal excitement, and an important element in the changing seasons.

It is no wonder that bird artists have such a special affection for the woodcock and its habits. In this charming book, eight accomplished artists pay tribute to this unique bird. I know that it will be much prized by everyone whose blood begins to tingle when they catch sight of a woodcock as it flits silently between the trees.

Philip

First published in the UK in 2006 by
Swan Hill Press, an imprint of Quiller Publishing Ltd

British Library Cataloguing-in-Publication Data
A catalogue record for this book is available from the British Library

ISBN 1 904057 83 7

Printed in China through Colorcraft Ltd., Hong Kong.

Book design by Giraffic Design

Swan Hill Press
An imprint of Quiller Publishing Ltd
Wykey House, Wykey, Shrewsbury SY4 1JA
Tel: 01939 261616 Fax: 01939 261606
E-mail: info@quillerbooks.com
Website: www.countrybooksdirect.com

Contents

Introduction

For centuries artists and sportsmen have been inspired by the woodcock; its shape, colouring and long beak stimulate the former and its erratic flight often frustrates the latter. To most of us it remains an enigma; a secretive little bird that provides us with few sightings in flight and very rare sightings on the ground. Those images are treasures that inspire the artist to reproduce and interpret it in a way that awakens the memories of the sportsman. That is what this book attempts to do. After a brief natural history of the woodcock, each artist has his own chapter. In it he portrays the woodcock in his own unique style and in a way that rekindles memories of seasons past. It is a book to be savoured by the fireside with a glass of whisky at your side and your dog at your feet. SIMON GUDGEON

The Woodcock
At a Glance

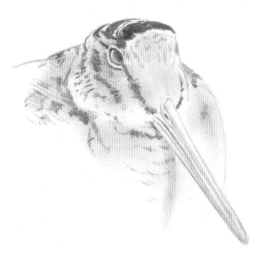

SCIENTIFIC NAME	*Scolopax rusticola*
CLASSIFICATION	*Resident and migratory wader*
HABIT	*Crepuscular and nocturnal*
LENGTH	*33 – 35cm*
WINGSPAN	*55 – 65cm*
WEIGHT	*240 – 420g*
LIFESPAN	*Up to 15 years*
POPULATION	*There is a resident population of around 30,000. Migratory birds can increase this number by up to 200,000 in winter*
NUMBER OF EGGS	*3 – 5 but usually 4*
INCUBATION	*22 days*
HABITAT	*Mixed woodland with open glades and rides. Plenty of ground cover of bracken and bramble with damp areas close by for feeding*
DIET	*Worms are the main food but they will eat beetles, spiders, caterpillars, fly larvae and small snails*
COLLECTIVE NOUN	*A fall*
SHOOTING SEASON	*England, Wales and Northern Ireland: 1st October – 31st January* *Scotland: 1st September – 31st January*

The Woodcock
A Brief Natural History

Iₜ's a mysterious little bird; seldom seen except when it is disturbed from dense cover in winter, and then only providing the briefest of glimpses before it vanishes back into the wood. That brief glimpse fires our enthusiasm and makes it a prize above all others on any shooting day. This book is by no means meant to be a definitive work on the woodcock; others have done that job far better than I could. However, a brief natural history will, I hope, give you a background understanding of its habits which will increase your appreciation of the chapters to follow.

MIGRATION

The majority of woodcock we see each winter have migrated from Scandinavia and the Baltic States. Driven out of their breeding areas by increasingly cold weather they head our way in search of a milder climate and soft ground. A good breeding season followed by harsh weather in October will lead to a significant fall of woodcock on our shores. Without that combination the birds can just trickle in throughout the season. The majority arrive with the late October full moon although some early migrants will come in late September. It is possible to see large numbers on the beaches and dunes in East Anglia and Scotland as they rest after the exhausting flight across the sea. As our winter weather becomes colder they will travel south keeping ahead of the snow and ice that can make feeding at best difficult and at worst impossible. Eventually they end up in the south-west where large numbers can congregate in harsh winters.

The exact origin of our migratory birds is uncertain but The Game Conservancy Trust is currently undertaking a study to analyse woodcock feathers to determine their origin. They will then discover if, for instance, birds that migrate to England come from a different area than those that visit, say, Ireland. If the regions they breed in have diverse weather patterns during the breeding period and therefore dissimilar breeding success this would affect the numbers that migrate to the different parts of the United Kingdom. This may explain why some parts of the United Kingdom have very good woodcock numbers whilst in the same year others have fewer birds.

Our country is not the only one that is blessed by these winter visitors. Their range is surprisingly extensive, from Europe and North Africa, through on to parts of the Middle East. They also visit Afghanistan, southern India and Sri Lanka in their search for suitable winter habitat.

RESIDENT POPULATION

As the light fades a weird noise is heard overhead, a bit like a doodlebug before its engine cuts out. It is unlike any other bird call and, like the cry of the curlew on a grouse moor, it always draws your eyes upwards in an attempt to spot its source. The male's purposeful flight pattern above the tree tops is so different from the erratic flight of the same bird disturbed from its cover in winter. It is much smoother as it flies around its territory calling to potential mates. From March to August it is a fairly common sight in the woods where a resident population of woodcock stay and breed. The size of a male's roding territory is dependant upon the quality of nesting habitat. A dominant male may control an area up to eighty acres whilst lesser males have smaller territories and will therefore mate with fewer females.

The female attracts the attention of the roding male by jumping into the air whilst fluttering her wings and exposing the white underside of her tail feathers. She will also utter a high pitched call. The keen-eyed male will promptly fold his wings and drop to the ground beside her. Courtship is rather a lengthy affair beginning with the pair flighting together in an aerial dance. This is followed by the male chasing after the female until she eventually lands where the courtship display will continue on the ground before the female flies off once more. When she alights a second time mating takes place. This brief bond is soon broken and the male will go back to his roding to search for another mate. A dominant male will mate with as many females as he finds in his territory and continues roding throughout the summer on the off chance of finding a female that might breed late.

It is the female alone that is responsible for nesting, incubating and rearing the young, the male plays no further part. She makes her nest amongst the dead leaves and vegetation on the forest floor where she will lay three to five eggs, though it is normally only four. Incubation starts as soon as the clutch is complete and when on the nest the female will become practically invisible. Twenty-two days later the chicks hatch by opening the eggs lengthways, unlike most other birds that pip round the side. I suppose the length of the bill, which even in chicks is quite long, makes it easier to peck their way out this way. The chicks very quickly become active although they are fed by their mother for the first few days. She will regurgitate partly digested food until they are old enough to search for small invertebrates on the forest floor with their rapidly growing bill.

If disturbed, the mother will fly away slowly, faking injury to lure the predator away from her brood. The chicks' colouration blends in perfectly with their surroundings and when they lie motionless on the forest floor they are virtually impossible to spot.

During the summer woodcock feed mostly in the woodland and often during the day to ensure their chicks get adequate nutrition. If they are feeding at night the mother will keep in touch with her young with a variety of calls. She also uses the white feathers on the underside of her tail to show her young where she is. These feathers are so bright that they show up in even quite low light and if the mother spreads her tail it provides an arc of white for the young to follow.

The woodcock that breed in this country tend to stay here and often within a few miles of where

they were born. When the family group breaks up in autumn they will leave the immediate territory where they were reared. Also, if the weather becomes harsh they will search out new feeding grounds close to good roosting cover but will often return to their home ground when it becomes milder.

No book on woodcock would be complete without discussing whether they carry their young. Those that have not witnessed it remain sceptical and until someone can offer photographic proof of the event it will remain a controversial issue. All I can add to the argument is that, although I have not seen the event myself, I have talked to enough people who have, to believe that it does occur.

HABITAT

There are two main criteria for woodcock habitat, firstly earthworms and secondly suitable roosting cover. In winter it will emerge from its daytime roost in the half light just before nightfall and fly out to its nocturnal feeding area in fields and open glades. The woodcock feeds by probing its beak into the ground, often to its full extent, in search of worms and other invertebrates so they favour feeding areas which have soft soil with plenty of earthworms. Permanent pasture is especially popular as worms thrive in fields where grazing cattle constantly enrich the soil with their manure. The end of its bill, on the top, is a mass of nerve endings so that it can sense the worms as it probes the ground. If it feels one it pulls it out of the earth and sucks it up. This habit accounts for some of the less elegant descriptions of the woodcock as 'bog-sucker' and 'bog-borer'. Woodcock have healthy appetites and will consume up to a third of their body weight each night in short bouts of feeding followed by periods of rest.

The feeding areas are usually quite close to their roosting area, normally only a few hundred yards away, and the woodcock will follow a set flight line back and forth at dusk and dawn. This habit of following this flight line facilitated the interception of woodcock on their evening flight by netsmen who, in times gone by, used to capture birds for the table. Their method was to set up a net between two trees on a known flight path and then when a woodcock flew into it the netsman would shut the net. This is the origin the term 'cock-shut time' to describe dusk.

In summer it will rarely leave the confines of the wood where it nests or holds territory and will search for food in the rides, open glades, and amongst the dead leaves on the forest floor. Woods which provide such suitable habitat are those where the woodcock will choose to breed. Mixed woodland with plenty of sycamore and ash are rich in earthworms and also provide the other essential ingredient for our resident breeding birds; plenty of cover in the form of bramble

and bracken. Hazel coppice, when properly managed, also lets in enough light to encourage plenty of cover for the birds as do young stands of conifer. However, as the conifers mature the forest floor gets darker and the undergrowth gradually dies off through lack of light. Beech woods have a similar problem as the lack of light during the summer discourages plant growth.

The management of woodland to encourage woodcock can have a huge effect on the population, providing the area of woodland is large enough. As already mentioned, coppicing hazel on rotation produces a diversity of habitat which is beneficial, as is the provision of wide woodland rides and open glades.

No research has been carried out to discover what effect deer have on woodcock. However, woodland with a large population of fallow deer will have a very noticeable browse line and much of the undergrowth, especially bramble, will all but disappear. This will almost certainly have an adverse effect on numbers of breeding woodcock as there will be insufficient cover for them.

AGEING WOODCOCK

There are no discernible differences between a male and a female woodcock and sexing them is only possible by dissection. Working out whether the bird is an adult or a juvenile, however, is much easier, although calculating the age of a bird after the first year is almost impossible to determine. After breeding the adult woodcock moult and by the time the shooting season begins their new primary feathers will still be in pristine condition. The juvenile birds, however, will have had their feathers for much longer and won't moult until the following year. Consequently the tips of their primary feathers will show sign of wear and tear at the end and thus it is fairly easy to work out if the bird is an adult or a juvenile. If during the season very few juveniles are shot this is an indication that it has been a poor breeding season.

K.J. SYKES.

Keith Sykes

Cocker spaniels were traditionally bred for woodcock shooting, their compact physique is ideal for flushing the birds from thick cover. Nowadays the sportsman hunts woodcock in many different ways: driven, walked-up, shooting over pointers and flighting, but the odd woodcock flushed on a shoot day is probably the way the majority of us bag our few precious birds each season. Consequently a large variety of different breeds of gundog are used, the main requirements being a steady dog that will work close to the gun and the ability to find and retrieve the fallen bird.

Many dogs, including cockers, have a great reluctance to picking up woodcock, avoiding them as though their scent or taste was unpalatable. At other times a fallen woodcock seems to mask its scent and the dogs find it almost impossible to locate, even when in clear view. Various explanations have been suggested for this inconsistent behaviour, one being that it is the odour of the preening oil that provides such an effective deterrent, however I have yet to be convinced that anyone has the definitive answer. Whether or not a woodcock can mask its scent from predators remains a mystery.

To date, I have not been presented with a safe opportunity to score the illusive 'right and left' when in pursuit of woodcock. I recall vividly an instance at the end of last season when two flushed woodcock circled a small plantation in opposite directions crossing in the air within gunshot and directly in front of my peg. Unfortunately I was not comfortable enough to shoulder the gun in anticipation of the oncoming beaters. What prize for two woodcock on the wing with one shot I pondered? . . . dream on.

On shoot days during the past couple of seasons I have carried a camera in lieu of the gun, endeavouring to photograph woodcock in flight. My success/frame ratio has been far from efficient, thank goodness

K.J SYKES.

Left
GERMAN SHORTHAIRED POINTER
Scraperboard

Opposite
'ON POINT'
Scraperboard

for the relatively inexpensive option of digital photography. I haven't yet managed to capture one falling to a gun but I live in hope.

For a number of years I have enjoyed some wonderful game shooting with my good friend Alan Wood who is the Shoot Captain of the Burton Constable Shoot at Hull. The Estate is a haven for woodcock with an abundance of rhododendron bushes and moist cover providing woodcock with ideal roosting habitat. This area of North-East England is a 'dropping-in point' for birds returning on migration from Scandinavian countries and in cold climatic conditions combined with certain lunar conditions throughout the winter months 'falls of woodcock' arrive on the east coast at Spurn Head and Easington.

These birds can be readily observed in considerable numbers whilst 'recovering from the trip' on the shore and reliable sightings of woodcock resting on North Sea rigs have often been reported. It is worth noting that only fit and healthy woodcock are taken as sporting quarry by the guns of the Burton Constable Syndicate.

It has been light-heartedly suggested by certain other 'sporting artists' that I have the comparatively easy task of depicting the woodcock in my artwork: invariably the ones I draw in the mouths of sporting dogs are dead and consequently very still.

Simon Gudgeon

For the last few months I have been trying to remember the first woodcock I shot. I can't. It may be the early signs of approaching senility although I clearly recall my first pigeon and my first pheasant, both of which were momentous occasions. My first woodcock should have been a far more memorable event as I probably shoot more pheasants in a season than I have shot woodcock over my whole lifetime. They are a bird to be savoured. The mere sight of one on a shoot day quickens my pulse and I go through the same dilemma as any other sporting artist – do I concentrate on trying to shoot it or watch every movement as it jinks its way past me, attempting to memorise the subtle wing beat, the angle of the head and the flick of the tail? Our views of woodcock are all too brief and never long enough to study in any great detail. A mere passing impression.

I do remember the first woodcock I ever saw. My father was shooting with a friend in the wood at the bottom of our garden. It was a lovely piece of natural woodland full of mature oak and ash with areas of hazel providing support for wild honeysuckle. The woodland floor was a mosaic of bramble and grasses with a mulch of dead leaves where the shade prevented anything from growing. I don't know how old I was but certainly too young to carry a gun and so I wandered along with my father beating likely clumps of bramble with a short length of hazel. When the woodcock took off I was not sure what it was; much quieter than the raucous noise of a pheasant lifting into the air this bird was silent as it flew off jinking between the trees. I watched as it fell to the first shot and then ran to retrieve it before the dogs could find it, in those days I competed with the dogs rather lined up on it and pulled the trigger, at the same time it jinked to the right. I was a very disappointed teenager. They are all memorable birds – and at times very frustrating!

As an artist and a sportsman I have a great affection for these mysterious little birds and the thrill of seeing one never fades. It is a chance to add more information to the memory banks which is vital to producing a painting or sculpture. Every glimpse helps build up a more complete picture of how it moves and behaves. A few years ago I managed to obtain the stalking rights on the estate next to where we live. It is a beautiful piece of ground on the edge of the New Forest; a mixture of ancient woodland and permanent pasture makes it ideal woodcock country. During the winter, whilst trying to stalk quietly through the woods, every footstep carefully placed, a flushing woodcock will often startle me as it lifts off close to my feet. One such occasion was the only time I have seen two woodcock take off at the same time and I was armed with a .243 rather than a shotgun! That was the inspiration for the 'Pair of Flushing Woodcock'.

On spring and summer evenings, whilst sitting in a high seat watching the forest gently close down for the night, the croak of a roding male woodcock will always draw my eyes upwards to try and spot the source of that unusual and distinctive sound. I am always surprised how quickly they fly when they are roding. I am so used to seeing them turn and twist between trees when it is difficult to assess their speed. When roding they tend to fly in a fairly straight line and cover their territory with great speed. Any waiting female would have to make her presence known quickly or the opportunity would be missed!

It is rare to see a woodcock on the ground during daylight. I have witnessed it only twice and on both occasions I was amazed how quickly they run. At night, however it is much easier to find them. A year ago I invested in some night vision equipment so that

than other guns, always trying to flush birds and then find them. I found it lying under some hazel with its wings outspread; it blended so perfectly with the dried oak leaves it was almost invisible. I remember being entranced by its long beak, large eyes and its beautiful markings. Carefully lifting it up in both hands I gingerly carried the treasure back to my father. He told me what it was and spread its wing to show me the location of the pin feathers, explaining that they were once used by artists as paint brushes. Little did I think that one day that is what I would do.

But I still cannot remember my first woodcock. I remember the four I shot last season (a good year); the fact that I shot none the season before. I remember watching my wife, Monique, shoot her first woodcock in a muddy ploughed field in East Anglia three years ago after I had missed it. I also remember the first woodcock I missed; I was on a hillside at the edge of a wood and it flew straight towards me, I carefully

I could watch nocturnal creatures without disturbing them – it is also extremely useful in keeping the fox population under control. Creatures are less wary at night and it is possible to get close to them without disturbing them. Deer, badgers and hares are all more active at night and being able to observe them gives the artist a far greater insight into their behaviour. I have called in a barn owl using a distressed rabbit call and seen hares pronking like startled antelope, but the most treasured sightings have been on woodcock.

When I first saw them I had difficulty making out what they were. Little blobs in a field with eyes bright from the reflection of the infra red torch. As I got closer it dawned on me that they were woodcock, and not just one or two but eleven in one field. The woodcock has often been described as a secretive and solitary bird. The former description is largely due to its nocturnal habit and the latter to the fact that two woodcock in the air at the same time is a rare sight. But here were a large number congregating in ones, twos and small groups of up to five. When I got too close they flew a small distance, giving an alarm call similar to snipe, and the more they were disturbed the larger the group they formed. For much of the time they were crouching down in the grass resting. If they were feeding they seemed to go off and do that by themselves. It was an amazing opportunity to observe them on the ground and flying. One woodcock was resting on a mole hill which provided the inspiration for the 'Sitting Woodcock' sculpture.

Whilst watching woodcock on numerous occasions on the farm where I shoot there is definitely one field that is a favourite. The farm is around eight hundred acres and it is possible to walk around the whole of it and only see woodcock in one or two fields, normally permanent pasture, and in those fields it is possible to see up to fifteen birds at a time.

I had developed a deep affection for these odd shaped little birds long before I became an artist. Since I started dabbling and daubing with paint and clay I have drawn, painted and sculpted woodcock, including painting them using a pin feather (a normal paintbrush is much easier). The first sculpture I ever did was of a woodcock and the first flying bird I created was also one. Its long beak and the unique shape of its head make it a wonderful subject. Sculpting birds in flight always poses a big challenge as it is hard to convey the freedom of flight whilst having to attach the bird to a base. My usual trick is to have the wings on the downward sweep so that where the bird is attached to the base is obscured as I did for my first 'Flying Woodcock' bronze. For the 'Flushing Woodcock' I wanted to convey the feeling of the bird fighting gravity as it lifts from the ground and show it stretching its wings to the limit before powering them down to gain height. The wings of the woodcock are surprisingly long for the size of its body and although in normal flight the wing beat is quite shallow when they take off they use the full flexibility available in order to get themselves off the ground. This posed a problem as I would not be able to use a lowered wing to hide where the mount joins the body. It was whilst watching a woodcock take off from rushes in the damp area of a field that I came up with the idea of adapting the rushes to form the base. Then it was the dilemma of trying to get enough strength in the rushes to support the bird whilst trying to keep it delicate enough so that it did not dominate the piece. Luckily when it all went together it didn't collapse!

As a sportsman my two favourite birds are grouse and woodcock. For the former you either need deep pockets or generous friends (as an artist it is always the latter!) Woodcock are different, they are available to all, whether it is a walked up day on a rough shoot or shooting over pointers the main investment is time. The rewards, though, are great; wonderful memories and, with luck, one of the most delicious of all game birds on your plate. As an artist I do not have a favourite subject but every fresh sighting of a woodcock brings new inspiration.

Opposite, above and right
RESTING WOODCOCK
Bronze, limited edition of 12

This was inspired by a woodcock I had seen using night vision equipment. It was sitting on a mole hill with three other woodcock close by, resting between bouts of feeding.

Right
SMALL NESTING WOODCOCK
Bronze, limited edition of 25

The smallest woodcock sculpture I have done, it measures only 140mm long. When I started sculpting it I was going to put in detail for the wings and tail but then thought it would look much better with very clean and simple lines.

Opposite
NESTING WOODCOCK
Bronze, limited edition of 12

I initially did this piece as a small bronze but thought the smooth lines and the simplicity of the piece would work as a life size sculpture.

*The first sculpture I created. I was fascinated by
sculpture but always thought there must be some strange
alchemy involved in creating three dimensional objects
in bronze. I bought some clay several months before I
started this piece and put it away in a cupboard. One
day, whilst tidying my studio, (something I don't do as
often as I should) I found the clay and started playing
around with it. I had just finished a woodcock painting
and so that seemed to be the most obvious subject
matter. After a few false starts this is what emerged
and I was hooked.*

Opposite and left
FLUSHING WOODCOCK
Bronze, limited edition of 12

Sculpting a bird with the wings up creates a problem when it comes to designing the mount. I normally do flying birds with their wings on the downward thrust so I can hide the mount under the wing. I had seen this bird take off from a rushy area of grassland and that gave me the idea for this mount.

Right and opposite
PAIR OF FLUSHING WOODCOCK
Bronze, limited edition of 12

These two woodcock lifted off close to my feet whilst I was stalking. It is the only time I have seen two in the air together.

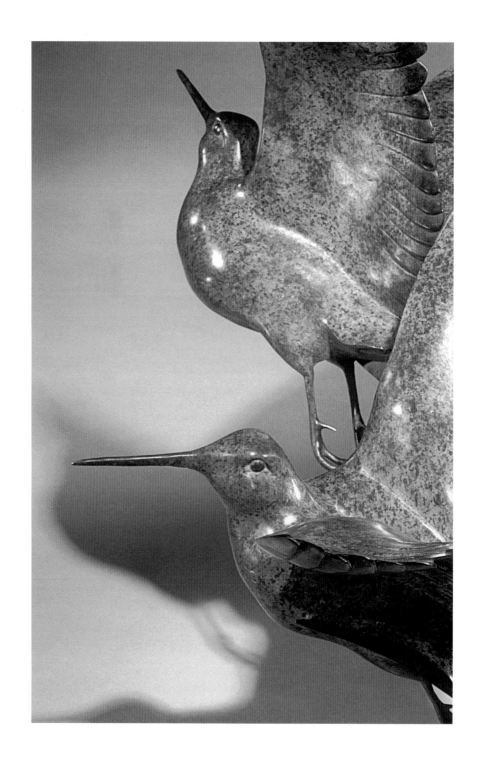

Opposite
CROUCHING WOODCOCK
Bronze, limited edition of 12

One of my favourites.

Below
SILVER CROUCHING WOODCOCK
Limited edition of 6

Ben Hoskyns

Dan the woodcock arrived at Colchester on the Intercity from Liverpool Street station, nestled in a box of shredded paper. It was the commuter train and the odd squeak from Dan attracted a certain amount of interest – eyes peering at Guy over reading glasses and the flicked corners of *Evening Standards*.

Guy has reached that point in life when he doesn't know whether to stick to insuring aircraft or become the Pied Piper of woodcock. They follow him around for no apparent reason. He doesn't smell much, or not of worms at least, and he is the sort of person who would fry up a couple of blackbird's breasts for breakfast, no matter that he had recently found the poor thing half-chewed by some errant cat in the corner of his garden. And it wouldn't be his cat so he would have to deal with that later. You would think, therefore, that any self-respecting woodcock would steer clear of him lest it should end up on a piece of toast – and Guy is the sort of man who thinks that

the trail is the best bit! He has a large collection of wooden calls to attract various birds and animals within range of his chosen weapon of the day and is inclined to use them out of context. So, there you are sitting out on the marsh, waiting for the teal to flight, and a roe suddenly starts barking somewhere out on the saltings. It is one of these, I suspect, that he uses to attract woodcock.

A few years ago, in late November, he was walking into his office in what was then called Commercial Union Square, just across the road from Leadenhall Market and next to the Lloyds building, and found a dead woodcock by the front door. His co-workers had studiously avoided the curious looking bird and, certainly, would never have dreamed of picking it up and taking it home to bung in the Aga. Which is, of course, exactly what Guy did with this manna from heaven. He, then, carefully packed away his woodcock call in cotton wool and carried on checking up on Aer

Lingus's No Claim Bonus. A year or so later, success was snatched from his grasp due to an oversight in timing. The woodcock arrived at the rendezvous a minute before Guy and, of all the luck, was spotted by an overweight countryman (dressed in a heavy tweed suit to prove it) who pursued it, huffing and puffing in a rather puce way, through the traffic in Mark Lane, EC3. Had the congestion charge been in place in those days the traffic would, no doubt, have been moving and neither the woodcock nor Tweedy would have stood a chance – a clear argument for change: think about it, Ken. Eventually, I understand, the RSPCA came to the rescue with a large net.

One lunchtime a couple of years later, Guy was once again about to enter the front doors of his office (insurance obviously involves a lot of coming and going). He had moved jobs and his new office was in Mincing Lane, EC3. As he reached for the glass doors, something brown and feathery crashed into them. Dan the woodcock had answered the call.

* * * * * * * * *

Dan had no idea what glass was but, putting the tip of his highly sensitive bill at speed into what he thought was wide open space, he very quickly found out. He had crossed the North Sea under the almost full moon of 17 November 2002 and, bemused by the bright lights of London stretching for what seemed like an eternity, had stopped to rest in Victoria Park. His sleep was finally disturbed by a questing labrador, in town for the week, who knew all about woodcock.

Bodger's owner, Julia, was flustered. She'd had a frantic morning getting the children back to school, sorting the plumber to fix the leaking washing machine and making final arrangements for the Church's Christmas Fayre fundraiser up at the Hall. She was 'doing lunch', later, with friends in London and spending the rest of the week there doing pretty much the same, amidst frenzied bouts of Christmas shopping.

Bodger looked on in a dignified way. He had barely been let out for a pee that morning but it was the same every Monday and it wasn't much better during the rest of the week. Julia was that sort of person. He hopped into the back of the Audi and they set off for the flat.

Endless roadworks made for a miserable journey and the Mile End Road was chocker. By now, Bodger needed more than a pee and was getting restless. Julia had intended to take him straight out onto the common once she reached the flat but it would take them more than an hour to get to Clapham in this traffic so she made a detour and headed up to Victoria Park.

She had forgotten to bring any plastic bags with her so she headed for the nearest shrubby area, praying that Bodger would hold on until he got there. Bodger was old enough to know the difference between London parks and the country. One didn't hunt in London – there was never anything fun to be found in cover other than the occasional half eaten burger. But today was different. There was a slight breeze and Bodger caught the unmistakable whiff of woodcock over the diesel fumes. As he bounded into the bushes, there was a clatter of wings and Dan emerged into the open, beating low across the path fifty yards in front of Julia who stopped dead, mesmerised – her hectic life

Right
FLUSHING WOODCOCK
Watercolour

suddenly calmed by the moth-like movement she had immediately recognised. Dan flicked his wings, rose sharply to clear a clump of thorns and disappeared. To this day, Julia's husband maintains that she was mistaken.

Dan flew over the lake and turned down Old Ford Road. It had all looked very different the night before, although equally confusing. He had no idea where he was and found the traffic and bustle of city-life highly alarming. A gust of wind blew an old plastic bag high into the air in front of him and he turned sharply down Cambridge Heath Road. Wailing Police sirens and flashing lights in the Mile End Road shepherded him down Whitechapel. He flew twice around Aldgate, unsure of which exit to take and suddenly darted off down the smaller roads. He calmed down a little and started to look for somewhere to stop, his big eyes swivelling down every street in search of something that vaguely resembled home.

He spotted some shrubs and decided to take a breather when, suddenly, he saw another woodcock coming towards him. Things were looking up although his new-found friend was playing some suicidal game of dare. Dan chickened out first. Should have waited: the other bird dodged in the same direction and they hit each other more or less head on.

Dan had been too preoccupied with trying to avoid the other woodcock to have paid much attention to Guy and was too dazed to do so after the collision or he might have noticed the be-suited fellow slip the wooden call into his pocket. All Dan knew was that he had come off worst - the other bird had already pushed off.

When he realised that Dan was still alive - his eyes were spinning and, when he came to, he staggered about like a drunk - Guy carried him to a nearby flower bed, hoping that he would recover, although his stomach had other, altogether darker, thoughts. But his gentleness went down well with the shrieking secretaries who surrounded him, asking what the strange bird was. It was at this point that Guy rang me, knowing that I had looked after a woodcock once before.

* * * * * * * * *

My first labrador, Towser, rather enjoyed hunting for woodcock and would come up on point, briefly, before trying to nail them. To be honest, he did that with most things as he had little faith in my shooting prowess but there was something different about the way he approached woodcock and I believe his affinity with them began when, aged only eight months, he disappeared into a muddy ditch and emerged with what, at first, I took to be a rat.

Towser had once been bitten on the end of his nose by a rat and made the most of any opportunity to deliver retribution upon its kith and kin. This honorary terrier status only involved rats (and once a young duckling, called Daphne, that he saw chasing us down the garden in a menacing way and decided it needed taking out). Well, okay, he was rather hot on pheasants, too, but only on shooting days. When he hadn't been asked to hunt, he ignored them and, providing the thing didn't struggle or bite him on the end of his nose, he could be surprisingly soft-mouthed – something I would often prove by getting him to retrieve eggs.

Towser's lessons with the dummy had been going extremely well so he knew exactly what to do and brought the bird straight to hand. I couldn't see any sign of injury but it was such an opportunity that I simply couldn't release it immediately. I didn't paint for a living in those days - it had been thoroughly drummed out of me at school and I had given up Art before 'O' levels - but I occasionally scribbled and loved taking a photographic record of the wildlife I saw. My skills with a camera, however, were not good but I knew a man who pretended to know rather more about it than I so I rushed it across to his house where he had a little pen set up in his garage. He took some snaps while I rummaged around in the attic at home for my father's old cine camera.

We quickly discovered that the bird had injured its wing, probably due to a keen pick-up by an eight month-old puppy who had initially thought it was a rat. The wing wasn't broken but it couldn't fly and clearly needed a little time to recuperate so we put it in the pen and I filled a shallow dish with some mud and ten or fifteen worms.

I had no idea how many worms a woodcock should eat in a night but the next morning it was clear that it was more than ten to fifteen. I dug up thirty more and put them in the dish. The following morning we found that a rat had got into the pen and killed the poor bird. There were no worms left in the dish.

Two years later, Towser caught another woodcock. We were out walking up hedgerows and he emerged with it from a thick patch of thorn and bramble. I checked it over carefully and could see no sign of injury so, asking the others not to shoot, I opened my hands and let it fly away.

I had one other close encounter a couple of years ago when out walking the dogs. I heard the unmistakable sound of a woodcock flushing a little bit ahead of us amongst a stand of blackthorn and looked up to see the bird hit a branch and fall like a stone. I sat the dogs and stumbled off into the trees to search for the unfortunate bird. I hunted for about ten minutes and found only half a dozen breast feathers. Eventually, I went back to the dogs waiting for me on the ride to carry on with our walk and, ten yards further on, the woodcock rose again and flew off. Clearly, it had been dazed rather than completely stunned and had been able to run off and hide and, by the time I had given up looking for it, it had fully recovered.

At the time of Dan's arrival, I had been painting professionally for over fourteen years and had been passionate about wildlife all my life but I had probably only seen woodcock on the ground on some fifteen or twenty occasions, each time such a huge delight but usually only a fleeting moment – twenty or thirty seconds at most, frozen to the spot, knowing that the next move would send the bird away. I have had a few more chances since and once managed not to check my stride as I walked past one sitting about eight feet away on quite open, mossy ground in an old overgrown orchard, here, at home. I had my binoculars, as always, so I carried on a further ten yards and spent a good while watching it. I would happily have stayed an hour but it knew I was there and wasn't prepared to move for me so I slipped away and ran back to the cottage to get my camera. Creeping back into position, I found that it had moved a few feet back into some old nettle stalks and the perfect photographic opportunity had passed so I sat back and continued to watch and absorb.

After a few minutes, a duck mallard, which had taken to the orchard as a potential nesting site because of the pheasant feeders, waddled up the ride towards me. A cock pheasant stepped across in front of the duck and, it being April, was spotted by the owner of the territory which stalked in from the other side. And they were all converging on the same spot – where the woodcock was pretending not to be. Something had to give. The territorial cock got there first and seemed rather startled when the ground erupted at its feet – I do believe it would have trodden on the woodcock, had it kept its nerve. An extraordinary image to have all in one frame and somewhat unbelievable, had I tried to paint it.

In the circumstances, Dan was rather an opportunity for a wildlife artist who had spent a considerable amount of time painting woodcock. Dead specimens were okay but a real live bird was invaluable. Guy explained that he would check on the bird when he left the office that evening. Would I be interested in looking after it if it hadn't already flown? Without any hesitation: 'Yup'.

We transferred him to a box which I put in the back of my truck. I frequently kept wheat there and I knew that the rats couldn't get in. I dug up some worms and put them in a jam jar with a little mud, gave him some leaves to nestle into and left him alone for the night. I hadn't thought much further than that.

Dan was the name we settled on after asking for suggestions from our children, having initially rejected Woody as too obvious and Celia as somewhat implausible. It wasn't, perhaps, perfect but it was a good, solid name and we realised that the game could go on for rather a long time.

The next day, I tried to photograph the bird through the mesh lid into the dark and gloomy box and realised that I had to make the most of this fantastic opportunity. I dismantled two old picture frames and used the glass to make a triangular enclosure, against the end wall, on my studio desk. The sides were three feet long and the huge studio window, just above, lit it perfectly. I put corrugated card as a base in case the work surface was too slippery and covered this with leaves. There were two jam jars – one food, one water – and I wedged them both into a corner with a couple of bricks so they couldn't be pushed over. This, also, allowed Dan to stand with his feet level with the top of the mud in the jar and therefore feed in a more natural position.

Without handling a bird, it is very difficult to judge its condition and I didn't want to add to Dan's stress, which would just as likely kill him as not eating. But I wanted to be reassured that he was eating so I left him alone for much of the day and crept up to the window now and again to see if I could catch him at it. Each

time I looked, I would see him standing in the same position and by the end of the day I was pretty well convinced that he had neither moved nor eaten. Two days without food. How long could a woodcock last without eating?

The following day I turned out the jar and found a knot of worms at the bottom. There looked to be considerably less than I had dug up but I hadn't counted them 'in' so I couldn't be sure and, in any event, I could see several dried-up worms on the corrugated card that had managed to escape from the jar and had no idea whether there were others under the leaves. I refilled the jar with another twenty-five worms and, when I put my hand in to return it, Dan finally became animated for a few minutes. He walked up to the jar and prodded the earth several times. Having never seen a woodcock eat before, I couldn't be sure whether he had, surreptitiously, managed to slip a worm down and, in hindsight, it is clear that he hadn't. But, after each probing, he would dunk his bill in the water to wash it or drink – again, I couldn't tell which but it proved, at least, that he knew it was there. Then he returned to his living statue impression. It was as though he had been switched off and I didn't see him move again that day.

There was a similar knot of worms at the bottom of the jar on day three but, this time, when I returned it to the enclosure he livened up, again, and finally ate in front of me. He probed the mud several times, pausing to feel the direction of any movement thus working his way towards it until the tip of his bill hit the prize. After a little bit of grappling, he pulled out of the mud and scoffed the worm. After a couple more failed attempts and a little bill-washing, he shut down once more. I worked for the rest of the day within a couple of feet of him, getting up and down and turning over the large sheets of my sketchbook without, apparently, alarming him in the slightest. I timed him once for two hours when he did not move a muscle. I didn't see him blink and if I got up suddenly, his head wouldn't even turn a millimetre.

I think he had, more or less, gone into a shut-down mode. He was unsure of what was going on in general and about the supply of food in particular and had decided to conserve as much energy as possible. I don't think it was a camouflage thing – 'if I stay still, he won't know I'm here' – as he made no effort to settle down amongst the leaves and use that remarkable plumage to its greatest effect. Dan spent two weeks on my studio desk and never once sat down. But then birds don't often sit so, perhaps, there's nothing particularly odd in that.

On the morning of the fifth day I turned out the jar to find that Dan had eaten all twenty-five worms and I began to feel a little more confident about his prospects. For the next two days I continued to dig up twenty-five to thirty worms a night. It then occurred to me that, if he was finishing them every night, he might want more and so, during the second week, I began to increase the number each night and every morning found that he had scoffed the lot. For the last three or four days I was giving him fifty worms a night. These were, mostly, big lobworms and I threw in the smaller ones as a bonus, generally without counting them. I discovered all the best places for worms in our garden but it still took a while and sometimes, when I had been unable to dig for them during the day, standing out in the rain after dark with a spade in my hand and a torch in my mouth, getting covered in mud, it wasn't a whole lot of fun. Several people told me that there are simpler ways to extract worms from your lawn but none of them knew exactly how. Great, thanks.

By the second week, it seemed that Dan had settled in. Confident in the supply of food and water,

he didn't need to conserve his energy and became far more active in front of me although my presence never seemed to worry him unduly. He only fluttered up to the bubble-wrap ceiling of his enclosure when I put my hand in to replenish the worms and replace the water, which would become quite muddy overnight. He would frequently freeze for several minutes but, generally, seemed quite happy simply to potter about although he had a habit of tapping his bill on the ground every now and then, resting it there with his head held low. This was much the same as his initial pretence at feeding from the jar and I wondered whether it was a nervous action although he looked unbothered. When I replaced the jars he would show far more agitation – stalking about with his tail cocked or fully flared for a minute or so before settling down.

I think he used the water partly to clean his bill but also because it was easier to probe the mud if it was wet as he would frequently go from one jar to the other even when his bill wasn't that muddy.

Whilst I have no idea how many worms Dan would have been able to eat, I came to the conclusion that he was doing very well on fifty per night and that I ought to think about releasing him. I asked a friend, Richard, who has a splendid collection of wildfowl and other birds, about putting a ring on him and he suggested that it might be advisable to give Dan a week or so in his aviary to allow him to build up some wing muscle before release. On 2 December, therefore, I packed him in a box and took him across to join, amongst others, an elderly flamingo and a bunch of avocets. This was the first time I had handled Dan in two weeks and I took care to examine him carefully. He was plump and in excellent condition with clean and tidy feathers. There was a slight bump on the top of his bill, about half-way down, and I wondered whether this was the result of his collision but later examination of the photographs I had taken showed some with and some without the bump so it had

appeared at some point during his stay but clearly hadn't affected his appetite.

Inside the aviary, I pulled Dan gently from the box and put him on the ground. After a second or two he flew off, pitching in under some shrubs in the corner. He beetled up and down for a bit before taking up his living statue impression.

I rang Richard for a progress report ten days later and was told that Dan was doing well although there was a question over whether we should actually have called him Daniella. One night, Richard had turned his car around and the headlights had caught another woodcock on the lawn beside the aviary!

The dilemma, now, was whether to release him before the end of the season and run the risk of him being shot. We were shooting, ourselves, on 14 December. I could easily have said 'no woodcock' or simply released him after we had shot (although

we had a second day in January) but I could hardly expect our neighbouring shoots to do likewise.

Our first day came and went whilst Dan continued to cement his friendship with the flamingo and I finally stopped being indecisive around Christmas time. Dan had been in captivity for over five weeks and seemed quite happy so I felt it would be in his best interests to sit it out until 1 February.

I actually rang Richard on the second to be told that Dan had been found dead on 19 January. He had spent almost nine weeks in captivity and was

Above
STUDIES OF DAN THE WOODCOCK
Pencil

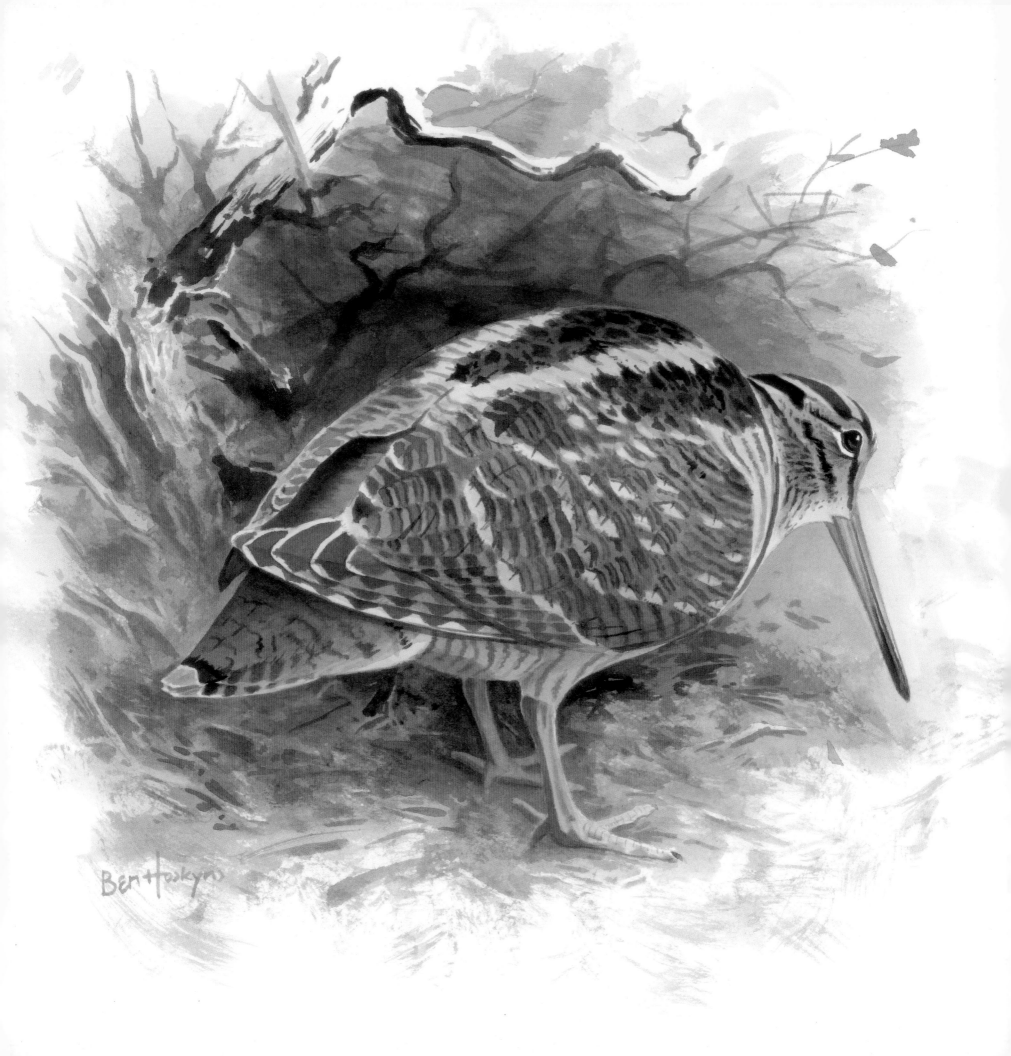

less than two weeks away from freedom and I wish I had released him earlier and let him take his chances – how wonderful to have been able to recount this story with a Hollywood ending. But I had been given the most remarkable opportunity for a wildlife artist. I can think of no other bird I would rather have had on my desk and he had been the most perfect guest – no mess, no fuss, no flapping about: he just posed. Rodger McPhail told me that I now have no excuse, whatsoever, for ever getting a woodcock wrong but they are still as tricky as ever to paint. The plumage is quite bewildering and before you know where you are, you're heading off in the wrong direction. Painting woodcock, for me at least, requires intense concentration but Dan has helped me to understand them a little better and he will live on as a result.

Guy had another encounter with a woodcock later that season when one ran across the road in front of his car on a country lane a mile from where he lives on the Essex/Suffolk border. Thinking it looked a little odd, Guy pulled over, dived headlong into the ditch and made an excellent retrieve. This one, however, was in very poor condition and, sadly, did not survive the night.

I still find it quite remarkable that anyone should have had four such 'woodcock moments' in as many years and that three of them should have been within a few hundred yards of each other in the City. However, by complete coincidence, Guy happened to turn on the television a couple of weeks after finding Dan and watched two woodcock, that had been found in similar circumstances, being looked after on Rolf Harris's *Animal Hospital* so, perhaps, it is not

particularly uncommon. Presumably, there are a lot of people who would never even consider picking up a stunned robin, let alone something that looks as bizarre as a woodcock. There are remarkably few who would think about what to do next and even fewer who would take the trouble to do it.

* * * * * * * * * *

Most shoots that I have been lucky enough to have been invited to have the odd woodcock and sometimes they have a good few although they are usually passing through and the day happens to coincide. I cannot, offhand, think of any shoot where I have never seen one but plenty where I only occasionally do. And, then, there are those where a handful always show and those where, come the November and December moons, woodcock are in abundance.

For years, the shoot here was somewhere in the middle. We usually flushed a couple and frequently four or five and these were mostly to be found in a boggy Alder Carr although, during the eighties, they were beginning to show signs of favouring other drives and there were certain shrubs and ditches where you could lay bets on flushing one. But when the 1987 hurricane blew, it severely damaged a couple of big ancient woods just off our boundary. These had, largely, been neglected for many years and the storm opened them up, creating a vastly improved habitat.

We hadn't suffered a great deal of damage ourselves, and I didn't think a lot of it at the time but we, pretty much, stopped seeing woodcock after that. I would see a few, whilst walking the dogs, around the time of the November moon and then they would disappear. I scratched my head for about five years, wondering whether it was to do with a change in the cover in our

Opposite
AMONGST THE UNDERGROWTH
Watercolour

drives or the increasing spread of pheasant feeders and the disturbance in filling them. I had just about decided – until a cold one threw everything into question once more – that it was due to the milder winters, when I went picking-up on a neighbour's shoot and watched seven or eight woodcock come out of one of the big woods that had been so badly hit by the hurricane. I hadn't seen the wood driven for many years – they only ever shot it on their last day and I was always invited to shoot in November – and, indeed, it hadn't been as it had taken them a while to clear enough of the damage to allow the beaters in. But the wood was only a couple of hundred yards from our Alder Carr and the woodcock clearly preferred it to our, largely unchanged, cover (and they had only, actually, driven an eight or ten acre block of it). I realised that I would have to wait until the canopy of regenerating and replacement trees closed up the gaps and made things a little less appealing. It took about fourteen years. Whilst it is still not consistent, we do usually flush two or three on a shoot now and sometimes as many as ten.

I have seen good numbers on a snipe shoot in Devon when frost has sent their little cousins away down the ditches, forcing us to resort to a series of short woodcock drives from longish blocks of woodland. They would have some fifty rises on one of these 'rough' days as they called them (probably because the bag was considerably smaller than on their snipe days).

I have seen a lot more in Norfolk on various shoots, especially when it is cold. A friend had a small, rough, overgrown marsh near Martham – half covered with Norfolk reed and birch scrub and half with alders and a nightmarish bramble undergrowth. Three or four of us would meet for lunch in the pub and spend the afternoon walking up woodcock and the odd pheasant. We always saw woodcock but, sometimes, they were really 'in' and we would have flushes every thirty or forty yards. We never shot very many as they rarely offered more than a fleeting chance but the whole place was always full of promise.

I have, more recently, been invited on pheasant days to a shoot bordering this marsh and have seen dozens of woodcock flushed. As the pegs were set back for the pheasants rather than close to the woodland edge for woodcock, a great many would turn before reaching the guns. There were no walking guns, either, to take those slipping out of the sides or turning back. It was run as a driven pheasant shoot and the woodcock were incidentals and yet they regularly shot twenty or more. The last time I shot there, the guns were limited to one woodcock each as they had shot fifty-six a couple of weeks before. They must have had something in the region of a hundred and fifty rises on that remarkable day. On the day I shot there, there were nineteen shootable woodcock from my peg and I shot the first one – which was unlike me.

I have worked hard for them in Thetford forest, stumbling down the piled-up rows of old roots where the woodcock tend to lie up, snapping at half-chances in the narrow skylight left by the growing trees on either side. Five or six of us have shot a dozen or fifteen head, of which less than ten would be woodcock although we would have flushed some thirty or forty. This has to have been some of the most rewarding shooting I have done.

But I have never seen so many as in 2002, when Alan Wood invited me to shoot on the woodcock day at Burton Constable, just outside Hull. Alan had commissioned a grouse painting which I was due to deliver around Christmas time and thought I might be interested in bringing my gun. They only do the woodcock day once during the season and, then, only if they are in good order and in good numbers – they didn't in either of the seasons 2003/04 or 2004/05.

I have heard it said that woodcock do not favour areas where there are a lot of pheasants but the highest densities I have seen have been on pheasant shoots and Burton Constable was no exception. It was 27 December but none of the drives we did that day had been shot up until that point, for fear of disturbing the woodcock, and they were heaving with pheasants. On the last drive, we were told that we could shoot 'some good ones' (although I chose to concentrate solely on woodcock) and we ended up with twenty-eight in the bag but we could have, very selectively, shot two hundred during the course of the day without much difficulty.

There were drives from short, scrubby or recently planted areas where the guns could just see over the top of the whole drive and from start to finish (in a drive that might last some thirty or forty minutes) there was barely a moment without a woodcock in the air. I saw woodcock land in front of me and run on. I even saw one running ahead of the beating line when it was still a hundred yards away. And I saw woodcock in the air like I have never seen them before with every bird different from the last, testing the limits of self-control and safety. Two guns had a chance of a right and left. The first missed his 'right' with both barrels and the second dropped his 'right' and broke his gun to reload when the 'left' emerged.

The final bag on such a remarkable day should not matter but it will help to give an indication of the numbers we saw:

94 woodcock
28 pheasants
1 snipe
4 pigeon
1 crow
1 squirrel

I was told that we saw sixty to seventy per cent of what we would have seen had the conditions been perfect. The day typically produces seventy to one hundred woodcock in the bag and the record is 138. These are figures that will upset some people, who may (or may not) be, morally, beyond reproach but I felt it was worth the risk to show what the place must be like. We saw a great many woodcock – probably more than most guns will see in five or ten seasons – and we missed rather a lot, too.

There were no oddities amongst the shot birds. There were no short-bills and, although the plumage varied considerably as it does with most birds, there was nothing out of the ordinary – all colours conformed to what we would expect to see a woodcock dressed in. But they have, over the years, shot quite a few short-billed woodcock and several light coloured birds.

I have always taken the time to look closely and marvel at any woodcock that have been shot. I have, simply, not had much in the way of opportunity to study and compare them in the field and feel it is important to note the differences. But, in thirty years of shooting, I have only seen one oddity – a bird that I shot in Suffolk last season which I have heard variously called flavistic, leucistic, bohemian and, perhaps most accurately, ginger. It had fallen, rather embarrassingly, at my neighbour's feet and, at the end of the drive, he bent down, picked it for me, walked the hundred odd yards back to the trailer and handed it to the man who was busy bracing-up pheasants. He hadn't noticed the odd colouring which was something that struck me the instant I went to look at it and I was surprised by his lack of interest. Most people simply don't handle that many woodcock during the course of a season; surely you would give it a cursory glance?

Incidentally, Alan told me a story of a Burton Constable keeper who was sitting up and watching, one evening, as keepers do. He had removed his hat for some reason and, as dusk descended, a flighting woodcock fluttered down and landed on his follically-challenged head. He came up with his hat but the bird beat a hasty retreat before he was able to cover it.

Woodcock have always stirred huge emotions within me. Even at the age of eight, as a beater, I sensed the excitement amongst the guns when a woodcock flushed. A pheasant was pheasant – very beautiful and all that but it did not require anyone to point it out. A woodcock, on the other hand, was greeted with great enthusiastic shouts and all eyes would focus on the covert edge in front. No change there, then. The implication that you are not as observant as your neighbouring guns seems to pass unnoticed. No offence intended, none taken and, for that matter, I'll shout 'woodcock,' too, for good measure, just in case my next door gun hasn't woken up.

I had no doubts, growing up, about how special woodcock were. With the added adrenalin, therefore, it took me a while to come to terms with them, as a gun, and, in a way, I am still trying. I know that they can present the easiest of shots – having missed a fair few of the very easiest, I really am well aware of that. They can be remarkably agile and have a mesmerising gear change one minute and the next they will flop out of a wood like a hesitant moorhen. You would leave the latter sort, without thinking, if they were pheasants but I know few who would leave an 'easy' woodcock.

So whilst I greatly admire those who, simply, choose not to shoot any woodcock, I am not yet ready to join their ranks. I have not shot hares for, probably, twenty years and have no urge to do so. I like eating them and we have plenty around but I just do not want to shoot them. Much as I love the sight of them, my pulse does not quicken when I see them out shooting as it does with woodcock and, I guess, once you have made up your mind, it is not a particularly difficult decision to adhere to. If I ever felt that I was a competent and consistent enough shot to make a difference to the woodcock population, I would probably stop trying to shoot them – there is more than enough challenge in trying to paint them.

Left
MORNING SUN
Watercolour

Opposite
FLAVISTIC WOODCOCK – HINTLESHAM, 2004
Watercolour

Above
WINTER WOODCOCK
Watercolour

TERENCE LAMBERT

Opposite
ABOUT TO FLUSH
Watercolour and Chroma colour on paper

The typical habitat where I see most of my woodcock throughout the winter.

Terence Lambert

The wildlife artist has some major life decisions to make – two eggs or one for breakfast, three minutes or five? What eight records to take to that desert island? And when you have dipped your brush in the pallet for the last time – to the deafening roar of your client's hands rubbing together, anticipating a hike in the value of your paintings – where to sprinkle the clinker? For me there can only be one place on the planet, the beautiful river Findhorn. I was first introduced to this superb east coast spate river when in my teens, and now with more than a half century behind me, I have not found a better place for contemplation or eternity! Over the years she has been so generous to me, giving me my first salmon and many exciting wildlife sightings.

The Findhorn valley has long been an important breeding site for woodcock. This woodland wader's grunt and squeaking roding flight is a wonderful aerial salute at the end of an evening's fishing. Two views worth noting have thirty years between them. The first, took place while watching a roe buck going about its business. The buck's attention was drawn to a movement in dense bilberry. I, tight against a Scots pine, couldn't move for fear of detection. The roe had walked upon a sitting woodcock that treated us both to a tail-up display – the white luminous tips of its tail being the most obvious, but confusing thing I could see.

Very late on a July evening in 2003, I was picking my way up a steep bank at the end of a day's fishing, when out of the woodrush at my feet flushed what at first I thought was a sparrowhawk carrying a kill. After only a couple of metres the bird appeared to drop the prey. The flying bird now silhouetted against the evening sky was no hawk but a woodcock. The dropped bird, almost as big as the adult, landed in the woodrush and went to ground. Searching in the gloom revealed nothing. Had I witnessed a woodcock

carrying an almost fully grown chick? On my return to the lodge that evening, in my excitement, that was the story I told. Since then doubts have tempered my excitement. In poor light, was the bird dropped or did they flush together one in front of the other? Did the young bird collide with the parent upon flushing, giving the appearance of being carried? After reading McKelvie's excellent book, I now doubt my first impression.

Everyone's bathroom should have a well stocked bookshelf. One of my favourite books for a long haul is a lovely old volume, *The Angler's Note Book and Naturalist's Record*. Published at the turn of the last century it is full of the most wonderful articles reflecting the eclectic culture of the Victorian era. Chapters with the surrealist titles, *Laughter in the lower animals, Fish and the salt industry in India, Sagacious dogs*

and *White kittens with blue eyes not deaf*, are ones the Monty Python team could have easily created. The book has only one reference to woodcock, under the title, *Food and the veracity of the codfish (1879)*: 'Independent of what may be called ordinary food, often very curious articles turn up in the cod's stomach. Some years since, at Flamborough Head, I was shown a pair of spectacles in perfect order and usable, found inside a North Sea Cod. On the 30th of October 1879, at the time in the great flight of woodcocks crossed to the English coast, a large cod was taken near Spurn Point which had an entire Woodcock in its stomach.' We don't experience 'a great flight' here in central Wales, but the huge areas of mixed forestry close to home are a magnet to birds flighting west. The first frosts of winter add a great deal of interest to my daily walks with the dog.

Preferred roost areas become predictable after years of walking the woods so regularly. Steep terraced banks cut into the hillsides to create the roadways, and open, well brashed, mixed woodland, give the roosting birds the advantage over the viewer. To see a bird before flushing is therefore rare. Flushed birds' normal behaviour is to break from cover going away, a couple of feet above the ground. Birds that flush late tend to climb higher. On one occasion pursued by a sparrowhawk the quarry evaded the hawk by a vertical flight, breaking out through the top of the larches. Small twigs were broken during the escape. When roosting deeper under sitka, birds will often flush vertically, creating a bit of a fuss. I am always surprised they don't damage themselves when breaking out in this fashion. I have tried very hard to find birds on the ground, but have only managed it on two occasions, both birds moving out of cover and running a short distance before taking flight.

A wildlife painter now for thirty-five years, I find the world of wildlife art sometimes rather predictable. I gain great inspiration and challenge from trying to capture the essence and to enter the universe of this enigmatic little woodland gem! Not afraid of taking chances, I believe that the ability to draw with confidence and accuracy is the great liberator, allowing the artist's observation and imagination freedom to create unique images.

Right
SIESTA
Chroma colour on canvas

Opposite
PENCIL STUDIES

Right
BREAKING FROM FRAGMITIES
Watercolour and Chroma colour on paper

Typical Anglesey habitat. A mixture of reed beds and willows.

TERENCE LAMBERT

TERENCE LAMBERT

Opposite
FINDHORN SALUTE
Watercolour and body colour

Above
HARD GOING
Chroma colour on canvas

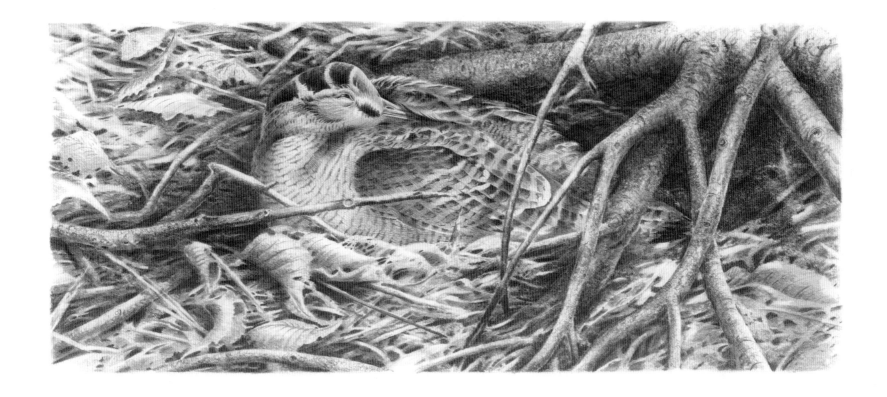

TERENCE LAMBERT

Opposite
PREENING WOODCOCK
Oil

Left
WOODCOCK STUDY
Watercolour

The ear of the woodcock is in an unexpected position, below and slightly in front of the eye.

Rodger McPhail

No bird poses such a challenge to the artist as the woodcock.

Its strange shape and subtle plumage are tricky enough to render in paint, but the greatest difficulty is studying the living bird itself.

Other quarry species are easy in comparison. Pheasants strut outside my studio window. Partridges can be viewed at any game farm, and woodpigeons feed in city parks within yards of passers-by. If a painter needs to study ducks and geese in detail, there are wetland reserves and wildfowl collections all over the country, where captive birds feed from visitors' hands and wild migrants can be watched from the comfort of roomy hides.

Even that wildest of game – the grouse – can be watched with comparative ease from a vehicle on moorland roads.

Not so the woodcock! The only time we see it is when it is in flight – or dead. The woodcock is a tantalising puzzle of a bird: mysterious, enigmatic and elusive. As a result, *Scolopax rusticola*, is seen by many artists, myself included, as the ultimate challenge, viewed with awed reverence by painters and sportsman alike.

I have had plenty of opportunity to see woodcock in flight. I see them every winter, hugging the contours of the woods on pheasant days. Sometimes hesitant and owl-like, sometimes corkscrewing through branches at speed. I have often watched them in spring, croaking and squeaking on their roding circuits, silhouetted against the fading light, and glimpsed them flighting out to feed against winter sunsets.

But when it comes to painting woodcock on the ground, it always comes down to a compromise – a mixture of guesswork, hope, and study of recently shot birds.

The fact is, I just don't know what they look like going about their normal business, and not many people do. They feed almost exclusively at night and spend the day in thick cover. There is no readily available film footage, and nearly all the photographs in the bird books are of woodcock on the nest – the only time in their mysterious lives when their exact location can be predicted.

I have on rare occasions, seen them on the ground, and these glimpses stand out as red-letter experiences. Once or twice in the headlights of a car on moonlit tracks or by the side of country roads on dark wet days. Once, a distressed parent woodcock performed a very convincing broken wing display at my feet. Recently, in Wales, a keeper told me that he often saw woodcock feeding in the pastures when he was out lamping foxes, and kindly offered to take me to look for them. We found several, and were able to approach to within a few yards as they were mesmerised by the lamp. One bird hovered, moth like, in the beam for some time, seemingly unable to break away from the light.

These, however, are rare isolated incidents. The opportunity to study woodcock as we study other birds just does not occur.

I never miss a chance to examine a freshly shot woodcock. The subtle beauty of the plumage never fails to amaze me. A human hand could never approach so perfect a design. The pattern of russet, black, buffs and greys breaks up the bird's outline in a miraculous way.

When I paint a woodcock in the leaves and litter of the woodland floor, I try to make them blend in with their surroundings as they do so well in nature.

Lastly, I love woodcock on a plate! Plump, juicy and sweet, they are a match for partridge, teal or even golden plover. The tender white meat of the thigh is a famous delicacy.

Above all other game, the woodcock deserves our admiration, our respect and our affection. For the painter, the sportsman and the gourmet, this reclusive and fascinating bird has no rival.

Right
DISTRACTION DISPLAY
Sepia

Opposite
WOODCOCK ALIGHTING
Watercolour

Above
WINTER WOODCOCK
Watercolour

Opposite
FEEDING WOODCOCK
Oil

Opposite and below
UNTITLED
Sepia

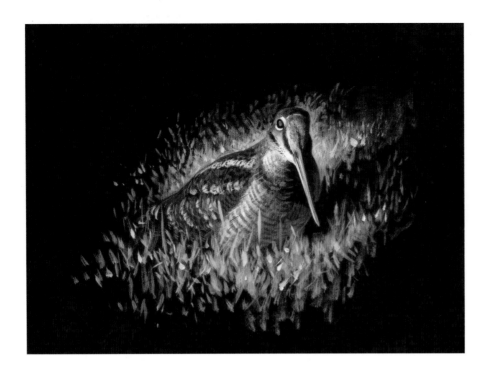

Left
WOODCOCK AT NIGHT
Acrylic

Below
WOODCOCK IN LAMPLIGHT
Acrylic

Opposite
WOODCOCK, EVENING LIGHT
Oil

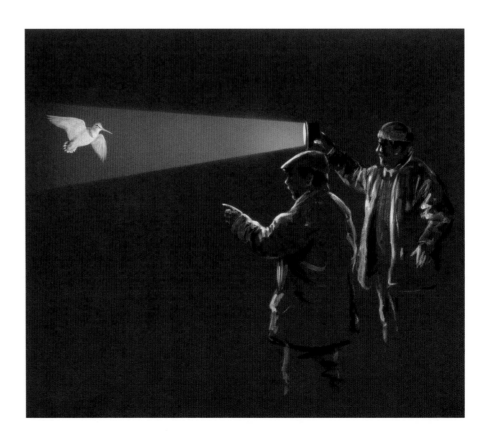

Above
STUDIES
Watercolour

Right
WOODCOCK PAIR
Oil

Right
OVER THE DUNES
Oil

Right
WOODCOCK IN THE SNOW
Oil

Below
WOODCOCK STUDY
Oil

Opposite
EARLY SEASON WOODCOCK – ALLT BLEAN-EIGIAU
Oil on canvas

The first woodcock arrive in our woods in late October to early November; the birds favour roosts below holly or brambles.

Alastair Proud

I can't remember my first-ever encounter with a woodcock, but it is a bird I have become familiar with over the years. In a way it is a bird one becomes tuned into yet due to its cryptic camouflage and secretive habits it maintains an air of mystery about it. I would have become aware of the woodcock as a special bird on meeting and hearing shooting friends enthuse on the subject; from this the desire to know the bird develops. In my immediate area of Wales the woodcock is not a breeding bird, interestingly it seems to eschew the south-western extremes of Britain for breeding purposes. It is therefore the end of October or early November when I see my first woodcocks of the season. These appear as the shadowy forms of the birds flighting out in the half light of an autumn evening. At this time of the year during the day the birds are found in several reliable places in my local woods – usually beneath holly or brambles amongst the fallen leaves. As winter advances more woodcock come in and one encounters them in different places. In hard weather with frost or snow they will be found feeding during the day in wet boggy patches. A good dog is very useful in finding sitting woodcock; although I have used a German pointer for hawking I have had very few points at woodcock. Occasionally while walking, one will stop for one reason or another and be startled by a woodcock trying to break free of the undergrowth virtually at your feet. Obviously the bird's nerve had broken and blind panic seems to take over. I have, with a hawk on my fist, seen the woodcock's large eye watching from just in front of me, body crouched and tail cocked ready to spring, the moment extended due to the hawk's presence.

The plumage of the woodcock is complex – and this is an understatement. Yet like all things in nature there is order amongst the apparent chaos. The large dark eye is usually the only noticeable feature with the rest of the bird blending into the leaf litter.

I sometimes seek woodcock out when there is snow on the ground and then the bird stands out as a darkened shape against the white background.

The woodcock is unique in its form amongst British birds; the snipe is the only other game species which is comparable and will feed in the same fields as the woodcock, however the woodcock will flight in and flush in silence the snipe will call very audibly.

Adult woodcock are predated by sparrowhawks, goshawks and occasionally peregrines. The two woodland species, goshawks and sparrowhawks, due to their habits are more likely to encounter woodcock. Trained peregrines are very capable of taking woodcock where they occur in open countryside. In Roger Upton's book *A Bird in the Hand* there is a fine description of a peregrine, while being used to hunt grouse in Scotland, taking a woodcock. Indeed, I have heard from a friend of a wild peregrine waiting on and taking a woodcock, flushed from cover by a spaniel working below; this incident occurred in hard weather when woodcock were forced into more open country. I myself have taken a

woodcock with a trained goshawk. The woodcock was flushed from a hedgerow while the goshawk perched in a tree above. The chase zigzagged across the field and the woodcock was taken as it put into cover in the further hedgerow.

Woodcock like roosting in forestry plantations where there is good night time feeding close by. Bracken between forest rides and streams gives excellent cover and it is a fine sight to see a woodcock flushed into low sunlight on a winter's afternoon. In hard weather the woodcock will leave the safety of its forestry roost earlier to feed in nearby fields.

As spring approaches woodcock leave my local woodlands and move east. The nearest breeding areas to me are the large forestry plantations in the east of the county. Here the roding flights can be witnessed as the first indication that woodcock are present and might be breeding. As the woodlands come to life with spring flowers the woodcock becomes preoccupied with its breeding activities. Woodcock usually have two broods of three or four young tendered only by the female. The fascinating question of whether woodcock carry their young is still debated. Anthony MacDonald, a shooting friend of mine, relayed the following story to me. A farm he regularly shot woodcock on was in an area adjoining extensive forestry. He frequently, when thanking the farmer for shooting permission, would show him the birds he had shot that day. The farmer had no knowledge of birds but would always show great interest in the shot woodcock. On a visit early in the season this farmer told Anthony that he had come across one of these birds during the previous summer and had clearly seen it carry one of its young. The farmer had not known that woodcock were rumoured to carry their young and it would seem a strange thing to make up! The carrying of young is done to move them out of danger for young woodcock are vulnerable to predation by crows, mustelids and of course the predatory fox, who will occasionally take an incubating woodcock.

Opposite
WOODCOCK CARRYING YOUNG
Watercolour

The debate as to whether woodcock carry their young is yet unresolved; however there do seem to be many eyewitness accounts that suggest that they do.

Right
FOX WITH WOODCOCK
Watercolour

Foxes will occasionally take sitting woodcock and certainly avail themselves of any pricked birds after a shoot.

Opposite
PEREGRINE CHASING WOODCOCK
Watercolour

Peregrines are quite capable of taking woodcock
where they occur in open country. Wild peregrines
will sometimes take advantage of a dog's hunting
activities, attacking birds flushed from below.

Above
GOSHAWK ON WOODCOCK
Oil sketch

Goshawks are very active hunters and are a danger to
the unwary woodcock.

Right
WOODCOCK FLUSHING FROM BRACKEN
Oil on canvas

*On a winter afternoon when the air is crisp after frost
the woodcock will seem a faster bird than it will on a
damp November day.*

Above
WOODCOCK PREENING AMONGST BLUEBELLS
Watercolour

*The woodcock will enjoy the early spring sunshine prior to the
activities of the coming breeding season.*

Opposite
WOODCOCK WITH YOUNG
Watercolour

*Woodcock are generally double brooded having three or
four young in each brood; the females do all the rearing.*

Opposite (top)
STUDY OF DEAD WOODCOCK
Watercolour

Opposite (bottom)
STUDY OF DEAD SNIPE
Watercolour

I have included this snipe study (Gallinago gallinago) for comparison with the woodcock; the snipe being the only similar game species.

Above
WOODCOCK READY TO FLUSH
Oil on canvas

A woodcock relies on superb camouflage but there comes a moment when eye contact is made and the woodcock starts to doubt its own invisible status!

Opposite
WOODCOCK FLIGHTING
Oil sketch

When snow is on the ground woodcock will flight out
earlier to feed or even feed through the day.

Above
WOODCOCK IN HARD WEATHER
Watercolour

When the weather turns frosty or snow is on the ground,
woodcock will be found in wet areas feeding during the
daylight hours.

Opposite
BRACKEN, BRAMBLE AND SNOWDROPS
Charcoal and watercolour

I wanted to show how the birds' brown patterned plumage makes for perfect camouflage against the woodland floor, and the snowdrops provide the seasonal element – spring is on the way.

Jonathan Sainsbury

I never saw a woodcock until I was a teenager, which is quite a confession for somebody whose childhood was spent playing in the fields, woods and streams of rural Warwickshire. My interest in nature was known to people all around. They brought to my door injured, dead and stuffed wildlife – but no woodcock. My dad was a corn merchant visiting farmers every day and was often given game – but no woodcock.

Was I unaware of them because other interests obsessed me? Or was it that the woodcock's nature is to be invisible? I guess in my case it must have worked.

My first sighting of this elusive bird was as an art student. I was walking with friends down the main street, called The Parade, in Leamington Spa. It was tea time on a cold winter's evening. This tawny bird flew slowly and steadily down towards the Pump Rooms and the park. Lit well by the early evening street lamps, shop fronts and car lights, all its features were very visible: its long beak, large eyes, its somewhat reptilian appearance.

Why was it there? Was it bewildered by the lights, a tired visitor being pushed further west to escape bad weather, brought down by exhaustion?

Or were woodcock falling all over Leamington Spa on their way back from the moon, which was the old myth that explained the autumnal increase in numbers before migration was understood?

My next encounters were after having left art school, by which time I had bought a springer spaniel. This dog and I walked endlessly. She, if allowed, would walk from dawn to dusk and I have her to thank for introducing me to the wonders that hid at my feet, for woodcock were among the many creatures that broke cover.

The dog's flushing ability inspired many new pictures, or at least, what seemed new and original to me. I was, of course, following in a tradition of sporting art, depicting walking up and flushing game to the gun. Except, in my case, it was to be captured with a paint brush.

These paintings came to the attention of William Marler who ran a very luxurious gallery in Cirencester. He encouraged me to do more of these paintings. He sold original Thorburns amongst others and wanted me to paint similar game subjects, so he took me to Scotland to source material. I remember the first time seeing roding woodcock in the birch woods of Speyside, especially on the back road from Aviemore to Insh and on to Tromiebridge.

On many subsequent visits made in April, there would be fresh falls of snow, which would make the pictures more romantic and beautiful. Also, the reflective properties of snow would make more light available to see the birds. (These birds fly much later than you think when roding, therefore a good covering of snow helps you see more detail and artistic licence makes many pictures only work pictorially when painted with a little more light in the sky than is usually present.)

I now live in Scotland where I often see woodcock. They are resident here and are seen when flushed walking in the woods, or roding in spring or caught in the headlights at dawn. If there is more than one bird in spring-time, a posturing display is often taking place, with erect, fanned tails. But I've never seen a young bird being carried or managed to find a nesting bird.

My strangest encounter was with a bird that fell to the ground with a 'thump!' beside me, while I was painting outdoors. The bird was dead, still warm and three-quarters plucked with a little of the flesh removed. I don't know what bird dropped it, but the incident happened around midday on a day in late spring. This makes me wonder how easy they are to catch, especially when I have read that in Shakespeare's day woodcock were thought to be stupid because they were easy to trap and net. (A stupid person was often referred to at that time as a woodcock.)

Before starting a painting I must have a knowledge and understanding of the subject. For me this means observing wildlife in its environment, making field sketches, collecting specimens of flora and fauna. From all of this come the ideas of what I wish to paint.

With woodcock, friends were always giving me pin feathers with the thought that I wished to paint with them, using them like a brush. This was frustrating because I really wanted the rest of the bird attached for reference.

One day, however, in Appledore, North Devon, where I lived, the local butcher, who normally never supplied game, had a window full of woodcock. I bought them all and studied them. Some were golden, others greyer, some well-defined, others less so. What a lucky chance encounter, to help me with my work!

It may seem a little macabre to jump for joy when finding dead creatures, but it is a chance for really close study, rather well summed up at the end of a poem by Laurie Lee called *Shot Fox*:

Now stretched, an arc of fur,
death drinks his lungs,
and in his eyes,
arrowed towards his den,
a blunted light ...

The child first found him –
dropping her hot-held flowers
for better things;
fell on one knee and stroked
his bitter teeth,
glad of her luck.

For this book, I spent some time with a gamekeeper friend, who organises woodcock shoots. He showed me some of the regular places where they could be

Opposite
WOODCOCK
AND ALDERTREE
Watercolour

This sketch is one of many made in a wood near me. It is a wonderful mixture of ash, oak, birch and alder.

found during winter. It would seem that year after year, particular clumps of willow and sedge, wooded rides and larch woods are repeatedly visited.

The birds lie up during the day on dry ground with good shelter and undergrowth all around, keeping themselves in a position to hear and see danger coming and leaving themselves easy exit points to rides and openings in the wood or scrub. Preferably all the places are pheasant free, wind free, quiet, with access to open pasture and unfrozen soil that will be rich in worms.

I am always intrigued how the camouflaged plumage of browns and ochres, that look so stunningly beautiful, can wonderfully imitate the ferns, bracken and leaves of the forest floor. They can vanish against this as ptarmigan in autumn do against rocks.

I can only respect this little bird quietly going about its business while most people are unaware. Long live *Scolopax rusticola!*

This page and opposite

Ideas for paintings taken from sketchbook.
Clockwise from bottom left: Roding; Posturing display;
Rock, bracken and feather; Springers and woodcock in
their landscape

Watercolour

In this beautiful landscape everywhere is soft and silent,
making the experience quite other-worldly.

Above
WINTER SUNLIGHT
Tempera and oil

The tempera is used to build up the snow and ice effect. Everywhere is frozen except the margins of the watercourse.

Opposite
SPRINGTIME
Tempera and oil

I wanted to show the richness of the forest floor in spring, and how light works, making one bird into a silhouette against the light and the other described by natural light.

WOODCOCKS AND RHODODENDRON
Charcoal and watercolour

In this picture I wanted one bird to be readily visible and the second a little more obscure, all bathed in a winter northern light.

Opposite
Ideas taken from a working sketchbook
Pencil and watercolour

Opposite
THE BIRCHWOOD
Watercolour

In old birchwood trees fall down and regrow, making
interesting compositions like this one. The woodcocks
twist their way through, helping to emphasise space.

Below
JUMP FOR JOY
Watercolour

A more worked-up version of the sketchbook idea on
page 111

Right
FLYING TO THE LIGHT
Watercolour

This picture is painted mainly in sepia colours, yet
bright, lightened areas are still realized.

Opposite
THE LARCHWOOD
Watercolour

Many woodcocks live in this wood. The birds that fly
to the light often meet their maker, whereas those that
double back into the dark wood frequently escape.

Owen Williams

Like most of life's great pleasures the shooting of my first woodcock came relatively late to me. My early years of shooting were limited by the location of our farm here in West Wales, which lies at 1000ft overlooking Cardigan Bay. Although I was brought up on the farm there were few places on our land that held woodcock and many of the better woodcock haunts in the surrounding valley were shot regularly by locals who had exclusive and well guarded agreement with the landowners. So my shooting was what one might call very rough, limited mostly to snipe, wildfowl and pigeon.

This is not to say that I didn't get the odd chance to fulfill my growing desire to take my first woodcock. On rare occasions whilst walking through a small shelterbelt of conifers on the farm a woodcock would flush from cover, but in my early years without a dog this came as a complete shock and coupled with my limited skills with a gun inevitably resulted in another predictable miss. So I was going to have to wait a good while to score. There were times when I thought that both pretty girls and woodcock had some sort of conspiracy against me; in truth living on a hill farm some miles from suitable habitat greatly reduced my odds in both cases.

I was fortunate in my childhood years to live close to one of Wales's great woodcock fanatics, a great shooting man by the name of Dai Morris Jones. A distant relative, he was responsible in part for my becoming a sporting artist with his enthusiasm and encouraging words for my early scribbles of snipe and duck. Dai Morris was a unique character out of a similar mould to Mackenzie Thorpe. He read every book on the shotgun from cover to cover and on his yearly trip to the Game Fair would be welcomed onto the stands of the great British shotgun makers as an old and respected friend. Robust in opinion and steeped in knowledge about all things shooting he was the sort of person with whom you could spend many long hours in deep and interesting conversation.

To visit Blaenbeidog, where Dai Morris lived, was a unique experience. There can have been few houses in the country where shooting had left such a mark on its contents and décor. People would come from far and wide to visit and spend hours talking about shooting. Prince Charles once visited and on many occasions when I called in it would not be unusual to find Dai Morris, sitting on a stout wooden box in front of the fire drying out his breeks after a day's shooting, deep in conversation with a couple of locals about guns and shooting.

As a youngster on my first forays with a gun I would regularly call in on Dai Morris, the small room in his cottage lit by a single bulb and the glow of peat embers in the open grey ash-filled hearth of his small fire. Often there would be a woodcock on the oil clothed kitchen table awaiting dressing and cooking once the reluctant fire could be encouraged to provide enough heat for the small oven to do anything more than its usual job of drying socks. The windowsill of his small room was littered with tins of gun oil and other shooting paraphernalia. His favourite Greener game gun would be left on the settle ready for cleaning and a wet cartridge belt slowly drying on a nail driven into the lime wash of the wall above the fire. On the Welsh dresser was a magnificent case made during the war years by local taxidermist Hutchings depicting a female peregrine mantled over a grouse with a stoat moving in to steal its prey. All three specimens were reputedly shot by Dai Morris, and the case was then commissioned from Hutchings who lived in nearby Aberystwyth. Pinned to the beams of the low ceiling

were pages from the *Shooting Times* illustrated with paintings by the likes of J C Harrison and a youthful and promising artist by the name of Rodger McPhail. In the corner there was always a wooden orange box filled with books on shooting and shotguns delivered from the mobile library

So it was in this room that I sat listening to great shooting stories long after my worried parents expected my safe return from an evening flighting teal on the nearby lake. Dai Morris spoke of days when red, and black grouse were common in the area, when the upland lakes hereabouts echoed on still winter evenings to the sound of roosting whitefronts and to shoot was to eat when times were hard. Of course all this was inspiration for my young imagination and a modest talent for drawing.

Dai Morris continued to shoot woodcock, or *cyffylog* as it is called in Welsh, into his old age. In the winter of his ninety-first year he took several outings with gun and ageing Welsh springer down to the Wyre valley, a good five mile roundtrip, working every patch of woodcock cover that over so many years had offered up their fleeting chances at that special sporting prize. Dai Morris died in 1996. Today in the graveyard of Bethel chapel here in Trefenter lies the grave of that great woodcock enthusiast. On the headstone is a fine engraving of a shotgun, a Welsh springer and a woodcock. There can be few gravestones in the

country that display a shotgun, particularly in the austere surroundings of a Welsh Methodist graveyard.

It was on one winter evening returning from a flight on Llyn Eiddwen our local lake that I saw my first woodcock. All the reading I had done, and confirmed by the many illustrations in magazine and books, had led me to believe that woodcock would only be found in deep cover under trees. Unaware of the woodcock's habit of coming out to feed in the open at night it took a while for me to identify a woodcock that I flushed on open moorland as I walked home that night. Silhouetted against the distant glow of the lights of Aberystwyth was the form of a woodcock that I had disturbed from its nocturnal feeding on open ground. With an empty gun and near darkness there was no time for a shot and anyway I had always pictured my first woodcock being taken in the wintery setting of that classic J C Harrison painting. Today was not to be the day; indeed I would have to wait a long time for that day to come.

I have always looked upon one's first woodcock as a special prize you have to wait for, as I did for my first salmon. The longer the wait the sweeter moment when it finally comes. From time to time a chance would occur and pass me by.

Being of an excitable disposition has done little to help my effectiveness with a shotgun. The sound of geese in flight or the shout of 'woodcock' on a drive quickens the pulse and dissolves any composure I might have. The forgetting of the safety catch or a poked shot is the usual result and this was the result on those few rare occasions when I flushed a woodcock on home ground.

So my first woodcock came embarrassingly late in life. I was on a shoot arranged by my good friend Simon Gudgeon at West Dean in Sussex. I had managed to bag a few pheasants earlier on that morning which had settled my nerves whilst surrounded by a team of accomplished shots.

Then came the cry 'woodcock' amidst the distant tapping of the approaching beaters' line. To my left came two shots then two more, nearer this time, the gun next to me fired and missed with two and then there it was flying fast and behind the gun line at tree height. With nothing to lose I fired and killed it with my first barrel. At last the long awaited day had come. I have a photograph of me with my prize, grinning from ear to ear like an idiot. It has not been shown to many but from time to time I dig it out and re-live that beautiful moment.

There it was, long after the losing of virginity, the catching of my first salmon and the shooting of my first Royal stag, I had just bagged my first woodcock, I will save the blushes of those who missed on that morning but suffice to say I was singularly unimpressed with such a poor display of shooting from those of whom I expected better.

Since that happy day I have enjoyed many special outings after woodcock, both locally here in Cardiganshire, and with friends in other parts of the country.

On one recent wildfowling trip to Coll in the Hebrides I was invited by Rob Wainwright (ex Scotland and British Lions captain) to join him after woodcock at Cliad, his home on the island. There are very few trees on Coll due to the distinct lack of shelter from the regular gales that batter the island. The rock on Coll is Lewesian gneiss, a heavily folded metamorphic rock that over millennia has eroded into very uneven ground of heather clad mounds and boggy patches in between. This affords woodcock good shelter in the deep heather where they will rest during the day before heading out to feed on the few fields on the island at night. The experience of walking up woodcock over heather seemed very strange, the one early season bird that Zala, Rob's vizsla, flushed for us managed to elude us but later into the season Cliad offers a very different woodcock experience for those prepared to make the journey.

One could hardly imagine a greater contrast to heather of Coll than the steep wooded valleys of Pembrokeshire where I have also recently been lucky to shoot.

Professor Colin Trotman is a familiar name to those who take their woodcock shooting seriously. Each season he writes a monthly round up of woodcock sport in the *Shooting Times*. He has shot woodcock since he was old enough to carry a gun and his interest in the bird can only be described as an obsession. Like all woodcock devotees he has spent years with gun and dog hunting the same patches of ground, so to be invited to share in a day's woodcock shooting with him is a very special treat. The deep cut valleys of Pembrokeshire see very little disturbance from man or stock being too wet and overgrown to be of any agricultural value. This is classic woodcock ground, not dissimilar to Cornwall, which is the reason why Pembrokeshire is second only to Cornwall in the sport it offers. This shooting is not for the faint hearted; with deep mud, brambles and dense thorns to work it is real spaniel country. You work hard here for your sport and when you get your chance you feel like you have earned it. This ground sorts the men out from the boys and is no place for the hesitant shot.

On our day Colin demonstrated the result of years of experience with what can only be described as 'instinctive shooting' a pleasure to watch even if it did make my clumsy and largely ineffective attempts look feeble. It is very heartening to note how caring devotees such as Colin Trotman are about woodcock and their habitat. Sustainability

lies at the heart of their philosophy, unlike many other areas of shooting where it seems more is better, most regular woodcock shots are more interested in the quality of their shooting rather than the bag at the end of the day.

Many of my most memorable shooting moments have been whilst out alone; undistracted by others there is a distinct feeling of tuning in with one's environment. Ironically with this solitary activity there comes the desire to share the intensity and excitement of such moments with others: this is the reason I paint. That said, the enjoyment of being out hunting woodcock with another of a like mind is hard to surpass. In recent years I have been fortunate to share some special local woodcock shooting with my good friend Luciano O' Donovan, a rare 'hybrid' of a fellow, as the name suggests. Our wildfowling seasons together are occasionally spiced by the treat of a visit to one of his favourite woodcock valleys where we've experienced some spectacular sport. In common with the other woodcock enthusiast I have mentioned he exhibits that same philosophy of restraint and an underlying deep respect for his quarry.

A few years ago I was commissioned by the woodcock aficionado John Tylor to paint a picture of the famous woodcock shoot of Lanarth in Cornwall. Woodcock have been shot at Lanarth since the mid 19th century and from the early 20th century it has been managed and run exclusively as a woodcock shoot. The mild climate of the Lizard peninsula and the perfect woodcock habitat of rhododendron ponticum and willow scrub make this probably the best woodcock shoot in the UK. For many years Lanarth held the record bag for woodcock shot in one day and still regularly records bags of over a hundred. Should all this sound excessive it is important to note that the Tylor

Opposite
RUNNING WOODCOCK
Pencil

Right
FLIGHT STUDIES
Watercolour

family manage the shoot to be shot once a season, and when viewed in this context can be regarded as highly sustainable.

Lanarth is the home of many famous strains of camelia and magnolia, which were brought to Britain and propagated there by the Williams family, who were the early owners of the estate. To this day the garden contains a fine selection of specimen trees including a magnificent grove of magnolias. Each year John Tylor, on the final drive of the morning, shoots woodcock standing next to his father's grave which lies amidst the magnolias.

In 2002 I was commissioned by John Browning, descendant of the famous American gun makers, to produce some designs for a pair of Browning 20 bores he owns. I teamed up with Peter Cuzak, the excellent gun engraver, to produce the designs on the theme of woodcock. Most engravers take reference from artists to incorporate in their designs, but in this case John was keen for Peter and me to collaborate fully on all aspects of the design. The process was fascinating with many meeting between myself, Peter and John.

I spent long hours working on the design, drawing the birds and fern leaves as a motif for the surrounding scrollwork. The final designs were engraved onto the gun's action and I have to admit to being very proud of the final result. There on the underside of the guns I have my name engraved alongside Peter's as co-designers of the engraving.

As an artist, woodcock have featured greatly in my work over the years. Any creature that migrates to our country from overseas arriving on a frosty moonlit night can hardly fail to capture the imagination; the mysticism bound up in this has inspired artists

for generations. The elusive and secretive nature of woodcock once here, only serves to intensify the sense of mystery surrounding this wonderful bird.

I have always been fascinated by weather and the mood of a place; many of my early forays with a gun were as much about feeling the moment as shooting something – just as well considering my poor shooting. Woodcock tend to inhabit moody places, corners where frost lies crisp on brittle winter foliage. Words can describe, but paintings get nearer the truth of such places.

Over the years I have been invited to give talks to local art societies and WI groups and have been faced with the question of why, if I love painting birds so much, I also like shooting them. This apparent contradiction has taken some time to resolve in my own mind.

I have a strong feeling about man's hunting heritage, which I believe is 'hardwired' in our DNA. My grandfather, who was a keen shooting man, once found a flint knife whilst digging peat in a local bog, where he also frequently shot snipe with Dai Morris. He was a writer and poet and was much taken with the notion that this was probably the knife of an ancestor lost whilst hunting on the same spot thousands of years before. He carried that small flint knife in his wallet for the rest of his life. Many would dismiss this as romantic nonsense, but to him this was a tangible link with his past, when that hunting instinct encoded in our DNA was essential to our survival. Today I also hunt to eat, although it is not essential as I can buy my meat from someone who kills it for me beyond my gaze. I enjoy the process from shot to table and consider it a worthy thing to do as it gives me a feeling of connectivity with the natural world. As Ortega Y Gasset commented in his book, *Meditations on Hunting*, 'when one is hunting, the air has another, more exquisite feel as it glides over the skin or enters the lungs, the rocks acquire a more expressive physiognomy, and the vegetation becomes loaded with meaning. But all this is due to the fact that the hunter, while he advances or waits crouching, feels tied through the earth to the animal he pursues, whether the animal is in view, hidden, or absent. The reader who is not a hunter may think that these last words are mere phraseology, simply a manner of speaking. But the hunter will not. They know very well that it is literally true.'

My relationship with the game I shoot is filled with respect. I am a conservationist, illustrated by the fact that I no longer shoot snipe here in Wales because I

Opposite
HEAD STUDIES
Pencil

Left
AT ROOST
Watercolour

believe the population has fallen to a level that can no longer sustain shooting. My concern is about the sustainability of the species, and not the individual; this is the distinction between conservation and preservation.

Despite being firm in my view I am willing to concede that, as I grow older, and hopefully wiser, my opinions may change. Sir Peter Scott, one of my heroes with whom I shared a love of painting, wildfowling, sailing and flying, in his later years laid down his shotgun and became one of the greatest conservationists this country has known. It seems there is a point in a man's life when the need to prove one's prowess as a hunter diminishes. It came to Sir Peter as it has to many. I am prepared to accept that it will come to me also. The signs are already there; I have a slight tinge of regret when I shoot a woodcock, the same as I do when I catch a salmon, recognition that despite being delicious to eat there is almost a greater pleasure in seeing them alive rather than in my game bag. But until that day comes I hope to be able to enjoy the simple pleasure of working a dog through frosty morning cover in search of that woodcock for my table for a few years to come.

Above
AT ROOST
Watercolour

Opposite
FLUSHED
Watercolour

Left
SPRING RODING FLIGHT
Watercolour

Above
AGAINST THE LIGHTS OF ABERYSTWYTH
Watercolour

Opposite
A FROSTY EVENING
Watercolour

The Artists

Keith Sykes

Keith was born in Morecambe, Lancashire in 1957 and continues to live there with his family.

At an early age his father introduced him to various aspects of shooting. Wildfowling, rough shooting, clay pigeon and rifle shooting in his early teens formed the foundation of his love of the sport. From ancestral links back to professional punt gunners on the Essex coast, the family tradition and love of the sport has now been passed to the next generation and inherited by Keith's two sons, Jack and Tom.

Whilst at school in his early teens Keith began to paint and draw wildfowl. This was particularly influenced and inspired by the work of Sir Peter Scott.

On leaving full time education Keith embarked on a career in civil engineering, eventually making a transition to detailed design in both civil engineering and building construction. Many of his early years were spent producing fine detailed architectural work on a drawing board but, with the introduction of CAD, drawing board skills became a thing of the past. Keith's latter years in the construction industry were focused on the project management of building and engineering schemes for the NHS.

Combining his drawing board experience with a passion for shooting and gun dogs he now concentrates on producing finely detailed animal portraits. Specialising in sporting dogs but portraying all breeds as well as horses and wildlife, he works exclusively in black and white on scraperboard.

Keen for an active involvement in conservation, he has served on the Executive Committee of the Morecambe Bay Wildfowlers' Association since the 1970s and has been the Secretary of the Wyre-Lune Sanctuary Committee since 1991.

As with many artists, photography has formed an integral part of capturing reference material, Keith is never without a camera on shoot days and his photographs often appear in the sporting press. His artwork is often featured too and in 2004 he was commissioned to produce the cover of the Christmas Edition of The Field magazine.

Simon Gudgeon ARBS SWLA

Scratch the surface of any wildlife artist and you soon realise that they all share a passion and almost schoolboy-like enthusiasm for what they do. It comes from deep within and most have had it since their earliest days – you could almost say from the cradle.

So it is with Simon Gudgeon – this country's leading contemporary wildlife sculptor. His earliest days were spent on the family farm in Yorkshire learning the essential arts of observation, evaluation, interpretation – how animals and birds behave with each other and in the presence of man. Learning to understand the importance of balance in nature and man's impact – good and bad. So it is in his blood, and since those early years his interest and zeal has increased, been refined and honed and with it his artistic talents.

Simon Gudgeon's signature style is instantly recognisable – a smooth, minimalised form expressing in simple lines both movement and emotion. A moment captured. He is particularly admired for his sculpture of birds in flight and the ingenious engineering of bases which seem to launch the bird into air rather than anchor it to the ground.

His latest work strongly favours an even more pared down approach to wildlife sculpture with inspiration springing from the smallest of details – the curve of a beak, the angle of the neck – and then moulded into a form which suggests rather than dictates a particular bird or mammal.

His greatest inspiration will always spring from observing in the wild. Simon believes that before you can sculpt a creature, you have to understand it and where it comes from. Relating creatures to their natural habitat and how they live within it are one of his passions.

He counts among his many enthusiasms a concern for the conservation of our fast diminishing natural assets and has long been a supporter of The Game Conservancy Trust. He is delighted that sales of this book will go towards supporting their valuable research and conservation work.

www.simongudgeon.com
sg@simongudgeon.com

Ben Hoskyns

Born in 1963, Ben spent most of his childhood in East Anglia where he now lives with his wife and two sons.

He adored painting as a young child but his art master at school offered him little encouragement and he gave up before 'O' Levels although he continued to 'scribble' from time to time – his subjects invariably being birds.

After several years in insurance, getting nowhere in particular, Ben decided that he had to move on. Stubbornly ignoring any well-intended suggestions that he should, perhaps, get some training first, he started to paint for a living in 1988. He had been fascinated by wildlife from early childhood and never seriously considered painting anything else once he turned professional.

Concentrating generally on British wildlife and on game birds in particular, Ben finds no shortage of inspiration whether at home in Suffolk, knee-deep in snipe bogs in Devon or dodging midges on grouse moors in Northumberland. His landscapes are, quite simply, about the feeling of 'being there' and his studies capture the very essence of the subject.

Ben wrote and illustrated Holland & Holland's The Nature of Game (Quiller Press 1994) and has illustrated several other books, numerous magazine articles and his paintings have been used as Christmas cards by both The Game Conservancy Trust and The Countryside Alliance. He produced the jacket paintings for two of The Game Conservancy Trust's Annual Reviews and for the front cover of the 2005 Scottish Game Fair programme and has been commissioned to paint the 2006 Wildlife Habitat Trust UK Habitat Conservation Stamp.

www.benhoskyns.com

Terence Lambert

With over thirty-five years as a professional artist Terence Lambert has illustrations in forty books and partworks, has had fifty-five different limited edition prints published and has exhibited more than fifty times, home and abroad. His work has been reproduced in greetings cards, calendars and porcelain.

'The Surrey countryside was my playground as a child and my countryman father my guide. Before my teens I could put names to most of the birds I encountered. Like all country children before me I collected everything nature discarded, feathers, bones, butterflies and eggs, all lovingly catalogued in scrapbooks and shoeboxes, and stashed under the bed.

'Through my solitary rambles I witnessed the predator, prey encounters that later occurred in many of my paintings. I joined the predator pack. Armed with a fishing rod, I pursued every species that swam in the lakes and rivers within bicycle range of my home. It was there I judged the weight of a kingfisher that used my cane rod as a platform to plunge at fry nipping at the discarded bread crusts floating under my rod. Daily visits eventually led to night expeditions. There were times when these extended into whole weeks away from home, having a negative effect on more academic studies. But it was opening my eyes to many of nature's secrets, feeding my appetite for new experiences.

'With a career in mind I spent four years at Guildford School of Art studying product design. Although never employed in the field, it taught me self discipline and an attention to detail, qualities that have helped in my desire to master the painting craft.

'So often painters are categorised because of a favoured medium or subject. I have painted birds almost exclusively for thirty-five years, illustrating the British list three times for various publications, together with a host of foreign species. So it's hardly surprising that I have been posted in the bird painters pigeonhole. When the illustrators' hat is put on the stand and the artist's berry is cocked at a jaunty angle, then the pigeonhole can be emptied.

'After the inspiration of observation in the field, I try to create paintings that are more than just accurately crafted. I hope to show the subject to possess a personality, not any buzzard, but a particular buzzard, that exists beyond the confines of the chosen rectangle. The plants and props that are part of the painting are not wasted marks of suggestion but are accurate in texture, form and scale. For the last ten years I have worked with both oil and Chroma colour (acrylic) on canvas. These paintings have given me the greatest freedom, allowing me to boldly cover the whole surface before tackling any detailed work. These works have freed me from my illustrator's mindset, an attitude that said detail was everything. Fine detail alone does not make a successful painting.

'Artists are a privileged breed, with many being able to choose where they live and work. For some there are opportunities to travel. I have had the good fortune to have been commissioned on projects that have taken me to the Himalaya, Africa, the Americas, and the Middle East. Although these travelling experiences have inspired many paintings, the core of my output has come as a result of choosing to live in Wales. The diversity of the mid Wales landscape is so very unique. Within a thirty minute drive from my studio, I have access to coast and estuary, mountain and moorland and some of the most beautiful river valleys in the British Isles, all of which are an endless supply of inspiration to me.'

www.terencelambert.com

Rodger McPhail

Rodger McPhail was born in Lancashire in 1953. He studied graphic design at Liverpool School of Art.

While still at college, he was introduced to Aylmer Tryon, and so began a long association with The Tryon Gallery in London.

Over the years, Rodger has contributed to many mixed exhibitions at the gallery and has had twelve one-man shows.

One of the great perks of Rodger's work is that it has taken him all over the world, and enabled him to enjoy some of the finest shooting and fishing available.

As well as sporting and wildlife painting, Rodger also does cartoons, caricatures, portraits and stage sets.

He has illustrated over twenty books, including two of his own, Open Season and Fishing Season (Swan Hill Press).

Rodger McPhail lives in the Lune Valley, Lancashire with his wife Cecilia, and his sons, Gavin and Alastair.

Alastair Proud

Alastair was born in Dublin and brought up on the outskirts of the city, at the foot of the Dublin Mountains. As a young boy Alastair spent most of his time out of doors in the neighbouring fields and marshes where he encountered all sorts of wildlife, from newts to owls and foxes. His first bird books, with the paintings of Allen W. Seaby and Roland Green, inspired him to combine his artistic ability with his interest in birds. He was further encouraged by having his paintings shown on television after he had sent them to a natural history programme called Amuigh Faoin Spéir (Away in the Sky). The programme combined trips to interesting places with their artist, Gerrit van Gelderen producing paintings and drawings of the birds they had seen.

Alastair left school in 1971 and left Ireland, spending time in Somerset, London and then Wales where he went to Art College in 1975. The course he attended specialised in wildlife illustration. Alastair found meeting students of similar interests and new ideas was the most beneficial aspect of the three years spent in college. During his first year in college he heard about The Society of Wildlife Artists and duly submitted and had work accepted for their 1976 exhibition. The work sold at the show and a commission resulted, along with admiration of his work from Peter Scott, the society's president at that time. The exhibition became an annual event for Alastair, but it was not until 1985 that he applied for and became a full member.

At art college Alastair had met Carl Jones who became a friend and introduced him to falconry (Carl has since become Dr Carl Jones MBE for his conservation work in Mauritius). Over the years Alastair has flown and hunted with most of the species used in falconry. He feels that to hunt with a hawk is a privilege and gives one an insight into the ways of the hunter and the hunted; the combination of hawk working in unison with dog is a joy to behold.

In 1990 Alastair was commissioned to produce the paintings for The Birds of Prey of the British Isles; a book written by Brian Martin (Rusticus of the Shooting Times) and published by David and Charles. A further book on the Wildfowl of the British Isles and North West Europe was published the following year.

Alastair loves travelling and has trekked in the uninhabited north-west peninsula of Iceland in search of Arctic birds, the gyr falcon and ptarmigan in particular. He has also travelled to Mauritius, at the invitation of Carl Jones, to study the endemic Mauritius kestrel. The wilder parts of the British Isles still hold the greatest appeal, and one of his favourite paintings depicted a ptarmigan in the wilds of the Scottish Highlands; this particular painting was accepted for the prestigious Birds in Art exhibition in Wisconsin, USA. Alastair lives in south-west Wales with his wife Jill, and two children, Tara and Conor.

'Alastair Proud paints with a depth of feeling that arises with an intimate familiarity. I have known Alastair for many years and have watched him mature into an exceptional artist. His portraits of birds of prey and wild country are for what he is justly famous, for few people are able to capture the personalities or the mood of landscape so convincingly.'
Dr Carl G. Jones MBE
Conservation Biologist

'Alastair Proud is one of those painters with the skill to achieve entirely correct detail without inhibiting the life of a subject.'
Keith Shackleton PP RSMA, PP SWLA

prouds@plasbach.fsworld.co.uk

Jonathan Sainsbury

Jonathan was born in Stratford upon Avon in 1951 and grew up in rural Warwickshire. He was fascinated by nature from the start. He went to art college at Leamington Spa and the Byam Shaw School and worked in the scenery painting department of the Royal Shakespeare Theatre, before graduating from Leeds College of Art. He has painted full-time ever since.

He has exhibited several times at 'Birds in Art' at the Leigh Yawkey Woodson Art Museum, Wisconsin. The gallery bought his picture The Game Larder for its permanent collection and toured his works round the United States and Europe. He won the Maude Gemmell Hutchison prize at the Scottish Royal Academy. He was a prize winner in the BASC painting competition. He was in the Sunday Times/Singer & Friedlander watercolour exhibition. His work is on loan to the Society of Wildlife Artists in Nature, Gloucester.

For many years he has sold through the major sporting and wildlife galleries, has exhibited at the Society of Wildlife Artists and contributed to numerous events supporting The Game Conservancy Trust.

Jonathan accepts commissions. His contact details are as follows:

Telephone: 01764 679011
Email: info@jonathansainsbury.com
www.jonathansainsbury.com

Owen Williams

Owen Williams spent his childhood years growing up on a hill farm in West Wales where he enjoyed long summer hours stalking the overgrown banks of his local stream fishing for wild brown trout, and in the winter months shooting snipe, duck and pigeon on his home ground.

It was during these early years that he first started drawing the wildlife that he found so fascinating. He speaks with passion about a particular evening flighting teal with a homemade decoy and how on his return home he set about depicting the moment in a drawing, the result was his first sporting picture.

On leaving school Owen moved to London to follow a career in advertising working for a major publishing company and although away from the countryside, his fishing and shooting, he continued to work at his artistic skills.

In 1985 he decided to return to Cardiganshire with his wife Sally and young family to become a full time artist. Many of his early paintings sold into the U.S. through the London Gallery of H C Dickins, and in more recent years he has become established as one of the country's leading sporting artists. Working exclusively in watercolour his paintings contain a strong element of landscape and weather, which help to convey a real feeling of time and place.

In 2003 Owen Williams was commissioned by the Royal Household to paint a picture as a twenty-first birthday present for HRH Prince William which now hangs in Clarence House. Over the years his work has been included in many major collections of sporting and wildlife art in the country. His pictures have been published in many wildlife books and the sporting press, and he is a member of the design panel of the Welsh Books Council. In 2001 he was commissioned by BASC to design their Wildlife Habitat Trust stamp.

www.owenwilliams.org.uk
wildscapes_2000@yahoo.co.uk